Systems Thinking for Sustainable Schooling

Systems Thinking for Sustainable Schooling

A Mindshift for Educators to Lead and Achieve Quality Schools

Edited by
Karolyn J. Snyder
Kristen M. Snyder

ROWMAN & LITTLEFIELD
Lanham • Boulder • New York • London

Published by Rowman & Littlefield
An imprint of The Rowman & Littlefield Publishing Group, Inc.
4501 Forbes Boulevard, Suite 200, Lanham, Maryland 20706
www.rowman.com

86-90 Paul Street, London EC2A 4NE, United Kingdom

Copyright © 2023 by Karolyn J. Snyder and Kristen M. Snyder

All rights reserved. No part of this book may be reproduced in any form or by any electronic or mechanical means, including information storage and retrieval systems, without written permission from the publisher, except by a reviewer who may quote passages in a review.

British Library Cataloguing in Publication Information Available

Library of Congress Cataloging-in-Publication Data

Names: Snyder, Karolyn J., editor. | Snyder, Kristen M., 1964– editor.
Title: Systems thinking for sustainable schooling : a mindshift for educators to lead and achieve quality schools / edited by Karolyn J. Snyder, Kristen M. Snyder.
Description: Lanham, Maryland : Rowman & Littlefield, 2023. | Series: Bridging theory and practice | Includes bibliographical references. | Summary: "The chapters include strong rationales for adopting a more natural way of thinking about schooling, one that prepares students for life as it is now evolving around the world"— Provided by publisher.
Identifiers: LCCN 2022034528 (print) | LCCN 2022034529 (ebook) | ISBN 9781475866391 (cloth) | ISBN 9781475866407 (paperback) | ISBN 9781475866414 (epub)
Subjects: LCSH: Educational change—United States. | Education—Aims and Objectives—United States. | System design.
Classification: LCC LA217.2 .S98 2023 (print) | LCC LA217.2 (ebook) | DDC 370.973—dc23/eng/20220831
LC record available at https://lccn.loc.gov/2022034528
LC ebook record available at https://lccn.loc.gov/2022034529

Contents

Foreword   vii
   C. Skardon Bliss and Janet I. Greenwood

A Tribute to Joyce B. Swarzman   ix

Series Editor Introduction   xi
   Jeffrey Glanz

Editors' Introduction   xvii
   Karolyn J. Snyder and Kristen M. Snyder

1. Systems Thinking and Sustainable Schooling: Foundations in Physics   1
   Karolyn J. Snyder

2. Expanding How We Think about Quality in Education   17
   Kristen M. Snyder

3. A Quantum Worldview of Responsive Power for Sustainable Learning   32
   Michele Acker-Hocevar

4. The Quantum School Leader as a Strategic Systems Thinker   46
   Elaine C. Sullivan

5. Networking for Principal Sustainability: A Chapter of Hope   62
   David Scanga and Renee Sedlack

6. The Beginnings of Collaboration in Schools: Team Teaching and Multi-Age Grouping   76
   Robert H. Anderson

7 Approaching Systems Thinking in Schools by Linking Quality and Sustainability: Moving from Theory to Practice 90
Anna Mårtensson and Kristen M. Snyder

8 Appreciative School Systems: A Path to School Success 105
John Mann

9 Toward the School as a Sustainable Global Learning Center 120
John Fitzgerald and Elaine C. Sullivan

About the Editors and Contributors 135

Foreword

Every so often when we reach a point in the evolution of scholarship in education and our approach to schools, a group of top educators from multiple cultures and countries applies their research to shed light on new perspectives about how to address critical areas of concern. And so is the case with this book. This time, the focus is on exploring the question, What will it take for educators and educational systems to sustain quality in schools?

Currently, we are seeing forces at work that could impact primary and secondary education in schools around the world for decades to come. In the United States, for example, parents are confronting school administrators, school boards, and professional educators over perceived cultural issues and demanding "sanitized" curricula and textbooks. The governor of a southern state has even signed a law criminalizing the teaching of certain subject matter in elementary schools and has banned textbooks politicians find "objectionable."

Meanwhile, educators are challenged by international forces to prepare youth with skills and competencies for contributing to a sustainable future. These foci and others reflect the complexity of schooling today and the challenges educators face to meet both local and global demands. As this book suggests, it is time to revisit the question of how educational leaders can create quality schools that are sustainable and prepare youth with the skills and competencies necessary for participating in and leading a viable future.

How many school administrators have had to wrestle with the official leadership structure as well as the unofficial forces in their schools, which are often conflicting and at odds with them? For example, the 30-year veteran department head who opposes every innovation proposed by the administration, difficult school board policies, trending attitudes, or a lack of commitment to the educational institution's success by the varied forces. Even the size of the institution can be critical and challenging for educators to sustain quality in education.

In this book, *Systems Thinking for Sustainable Schooling: A Mindshift for Educators to Lead and Achieve Quality Schools*, the authors give the reader an understanding of how systems theory can offer educators a framework to comprehend and manage the challenges of schooling today. They explain how positive and negative forces can interact and cause a healthy disequilibrium to stimulate change and growth. Their wealth of experience, combined with contemporary research, provides readers with concrete examples of how to develop and lead quality schools that are responsive to the complex needs of the multi-stakeholders and thereby sustainable.

The book pulls together the best ideas of the past and stimulates the reader to think carefully about systems thinking as it applies to the future of school leadership, sustainable learning, and the importance of collaboration in improving quality in schools. The book ties it all together with a scientific basis underlying the way systems thinking works in schools, a practical approach to the pressures of a political situation, and the importance of linking systems thinking to school quality and sustainability. This is the right step toward the future of education in the United States and worldwide.

Designing and leading schools from a systems perspective creates conditions necessary to sustain schooling in the 21st century and beyond. As an educator, transformed by the principles of systems thinking, I encourage anyone committed to the sustainability of quality in education to read this book. While "sustainability" has become a buzzword around the world in everything from water conservation to energy production, this book explains the underlying rationale for sustaining quality and learning in education.

Throughout my long career as an educator and ultimately the director of the Florida Council of Independent Schools, responsible for the accreditation and oversight of 160 private independent schools in the state of Florida, I have witnessed that schools are in fact social systems, not just static hierarchical institutions. The complexity of schooling, with multiple inputs and forces interacting at the same time, means that the traditional school layered structured approach to administering schools cannot be as successful as a systems thinking approach.

I encourage anyone committed to the sustainability of quality in education to read this book. This book is recommended for teachers, administrators, school board members, and any others in education. Successful school achievement can happen when systems thinking is applied to all educational organizations both nationally and internationally. This work includes the latest directions in a systems approach to schooling.

—C. Skardon Bliss, Director Emeritus,
Florida Council of Independent Schools
Janet I. Greenwood, PhD, author "The Greenwood System"

A Tribute to Joyce B. Swarzman

During the writing of this book, one of our close colleagues, friend, and Systems Thinkers network member, Joyce B. Swarzman, became ill with amyotrophic lateral sclerosis (ALS), commonly known as Lou Gehrig's disease. While her own chapter is not found in the table of contents, her knowledge, insights, and wisdom about quality school development are interwoven throughout the pages of this book.

For over 25 years, Joyce was the head of Corbett Preparatory School of IDS, during which she developed a systemic approach to leading schools to nurture future citizens. Her approach was crystallized in the M.O.R.E. Model (Multiple Options for Results in Education), which was designed over time from a rich research base on the best practices in teaching and learning.

Her strong commitment to child-centered learning drove the school's vision and mission to prepare children with social, emotional, and cognitive competencies for a sustainable and viable future. Her commitment to teacher training and continuous progress was supported by a culture of professional development that reinforced teaming, cooperative learning, multiple intelligence, global learning, and human connections. Her commitment to systems thinking was reflected in the network of leadership teams and peer learning that spun a web of interconnectedness throughout the school community.

Joyce is well known for her commitment to teacher training through the nationally recognized teacher training program SCATT offered through the University of South Florida for many years. In 2021, she was awarded the Edgar McCleary Service Award from the Florida Council of Independent Schools as the Teacher's Teacher.

Her legacy, as an educator at the school and university levels, has had an international impact over the last decades. Corbett Preparatory School of IDS has served as an international training center to promote brain-friendly learning and team teaching as core elements for sustaining quality in education and promoting a viable future. As you read through the pages of this book, we hope you enjoy the numerous lessons gleaned from the stories of Corbett Preparatory School shared throughout the book that exemplify systems thinking as a living praxis for leading sustainable quality school development.

With love and gratitude,
Kristen M. Snyder

Series Editor Introduction
Jeffrey Glanz

Why a new book series on school leadership, and what does this particular series have to offer among the many fine books already published in the field of school and educational leadership?

Research over the past decade has confirmed what many educators, policy makers, think tanks, and others viscerally knew—that leadership makes a difference for a host of dependent variables, including the most important one, student achievement. Additional research is needed, however, to more fully refine and uncover how, in fact, school leaders make a difference in a host of other areas. The answers to additional research questions will offer further legitimacy and draw greater attention to the field of educational leadership. The questions (which may possibly prompt potential authors to submit a book proposal) include the following:

What effect does the continuing increased accountability and high-stakes testing have on teacher morale, principal self-efficacy, and student achievement?
What additional information do we need about systems thinking and its relationship to school leadership?
What are the specific gender differences as related to leading schools?
What is the precise role played by school leaders in fostering inclusive educational practices?
How is social justice best fostered by school leaders?
What specific educational leadership strategies reduce the Black/White achievement gap?
How might school leaders implement an effective data-driven decision-making process in their schools?

What are the critical factors affecting high performance among principals?
What is the role of school leaders in reducing school violence?
How do leadership practices positively influence school-community partnerships?
What is the association between transformational leadership and teacher self-efficacy?
How does shared leadership affect school morale and productivity?
How do various types or forms of leadership impact organizational effectiveness?
What are the social, cultural, political, and historical factors that influence the practice of educational leadership in different countries?
How do leadership practices differ in differing contexts, social, cultural, or otherwise?
What are the theoretical and practical differences among educational administration, management, and leadership?
Why is an international perspective so critical for better understanding the challenges of leading schools in the 21st century?
How can school leaders address race and identity, bias and privilege, and racialized current events?
How can comparative research studies help us better understand educational leadership?
What can we learn from studying educational leaders beyond the school level (e.g., district and ministry [or board] of education leaders)?
To what extent does emotional labor impact educational leaders?
How can principals encourage action research and other alternatives to supervision to enhance teacher professional growth?
How do school leaders effectively implement new technologies not just for the sake of technology but to deepen learning and provide better support for teachers?
What are the consequences of workload on school leaders (e.g., the principal or others) on effectiveness as a leader?
What are the challenges that school leaders face in differing regional contexts?
How do school leaders develop the skills and knowledge they need to understand teachers' and students' needs and effectively guide learning?
How do effective school leaders balance administrative duties with instructional priorities?
What new educational management strategies can help teachers better confront classroom behavioral issues?
How do school leaders coordinate curriculum and instructional initiatives across schools?

Given time and budget constraints, how can school leaders find the resources to support an artful education (music, dance, creative writing, etc.) for all students?

How do increased efforts to promote teacher leadership impact the work of principals and their assistants?

What new innovative ideas can principals implement to deal with the increasingly complex landscape of curriculum today?

How can principals support teacher-led professional development?

What is the role of identity in fostering principal self-efficacy?

How can school leaders help schools become more integral to their surrounding communities—and how can they better leverage community resources and connections to support their students and teachers?

How can we better balance interest and work in instructional leadership with other important leadership responsibilities?

How can districts support assistant principals and prepare new principals as they take the helm of the school?

How do we induct and sustain good principals?

How can we best prepare future school leaders?

Most fundamentally, the Bridging Theory and Practice Series is premised on the need to connect theory to practice. Each of these questions rely on a sound theoretical base that has important, if not critical relevance to the world of practice. This international series, in other words, reflects the latest cutting-edge theories and practices in school leadership that attempt to bridge the perennial divide between theory and practice.

Although we look to publish manuscripts that have relevance to an international audience, we will accept more localized research that might only be applicable in a specific context. The manuscript, of course, must meet the rigors of academic research and have significant impact on practice. Feel free to query the series editor to react to any ideas.

The series motto is framed after Kurt Lewin's famous statement, and we paraphrase, that there is no sound theory without practice and no good practice that is not framed on some theory. Authors are expected to illustrate the intimate and integral connection between the two divides. In this respect, we are unique because we do not accept proposals that are "heavy" on one side or the other; rather we look for manuscripts that are intellectually engaging, with a sound theoretical base, yet firmly grounded in the daily lives of school leaders. I welcome readers to join the effort to increase knowledge in our field and affect daily school practice by submitting a proposal on any of the topics mentioned above, or any other relevant ones. Feel free to communicate with the series editor via email at yosglanz@gmail.com

As series editor, I would like to take this opportunity to thank my latest advisory board, listed below, for their efforts in seeing the series to fruition. Their feedback to the authors and the editor was instrumental in crafting a well-researched, practical, and readable volume.

Köksal Banoğlu, chief project executive at Maltepe District Governorship, Istanbul, Turkey
Clair T. Berube, Virginia Wesleyan University–Virginia Beach, VA, United States
Yin Cheong Cheng, Education University of Hong Kong–Tai Po, Hong Kong
Mary Lynne Derrington, University of Tennessee, Knoxville, TN, United States
Sedat Gumus, Necmettin Erbakan University–Konya, Turkey
Sonya D. Hayes, University of Tennessee–Knoxville, TN, United States
Helen M. Hazi, West Virginia University at Morgantown, WV, United States
Albert Jimenez, Kennesaw State University–Kennesaw, GA, United States
Benjamin Kutsyuruba, Queen's University–Kingston, ON, Canada
Orly Shapira-Lishchinsky, Bar Ilan University–Ramat Gan, Israel
Jane Wilkinson, Monash University–Victoria, Australia

Special acknowledgment is extended to Tom Koerner (vice president and publisher for education issues) and Kira Hall (assistant editor) for their support. I hope this volume and the series will receive wide acknowledgment for making a difference in the field of educational leadership.

* * *

As series editor, I am excited to introduce this latest volume of our series coedited by Karolyn Snyder and Kristen M. Snyder, both with a wealth of experience in the field of educational leadership, especially, in this context, helping leaders foster schools as sustainable quality organizations. Kristen is well known in international forums for her unswerving commitment to excellence in schooling at all levels and contexts. Karolyn is a world-renowned educator. She worked with schools and universities around the world to prepare students as competent and caring global citizens. On a personal level, when I first entered the field of higher education, she was one of the individuals who inspired me. Her mentorship and support meant so much to me, for which I am unendingly grateful.

I am confident that this work on systems thinking will find a receptive audience worldwide. Although there are a few other works on this topic, the editors have made a unique contribution above and beyond others. They have masterfully combined the vast research and work on systems thinking with stories from the field that give readers a deep understanding of the practical ways to enhance networking and realign school organizations to function as a system, which is key to sustainable schooling.

I believe *Systems Thinking for Sustainable Schooling: A Mindshift for Educators to Lead and Achieve Quality in Schools* will become "the" work on systems thinking for all prospective and current school leaders. This book is an important contribution to our field, and on behalf of the advisory board, I thank the editors and the committed and talented contributors for a work that will certainly make its mark.

Books already published in the Series:

Brown, K. (2011). *Preparing future leaders for social justice, equity, and excellence: Bridging theory and practice through a transformative andragogy* (first edition). Rowman & Littlefield.

Brown, K., & Shaked, H. (2018). *Preparing future leaders for social justice: Bridging theory and practice through a transformative andragogy* (second edition). Rowman & Littlefield.

Glanz, J. (Ed.). (2021). *Crisis and pandemic leadership: Implications for meeting the needs of students, teachers, and parents*. Rowman & Littlefield.

Stader, D. (2012). *Leadership for a culture of school safety: Linking theory to practice*. Rowman & Littlefield.

Zepeda, S. J. (Ed.). (2018). *The job-embedded nature of coaching: Lessons and insights for school leaders*. Rowman & Littlefield.

Zepeda, S. J. (Ed.). (2018). *Making learning job-embedded: Cases from the field of educational leadership*. Rowman & Littlefield.

Zepeda, S. J. (Ed.). (2008). *Real world supervision: Adapting theory to practice*. Rowman & Littlefield.

Editors' Introduction
Karolyn J. Snyder and Kristen M. Snyder

This book began with a query among friends and colleagues who have been connected over many decades around the topic of "systems thinking as a way of life" for schools and school districts. We have all led schools and/or school districts, taught in educational leadership or quality management programs at universities, or functioned as the vice chancellor of a state university system. The question posed initially to each author of this book was this: *Do you believe schooling is on a sustainable course today, worldwide?* The response from each person was the same: "NO."

Our careers had been built on the big idea of systems thinking where people, programs, and services are integrated and function interdependently around a common purpose. Yet we all agreed that little evidence exists in education today for the growth of a systemic way of leading schools and school districts, or for the governing agencies or those providing resources. How can this be the case in 2022 when new forms of working, leading, and managing are being invented daily, where people learn how to thrive within and across organizational units, sectors, companies, and regions of the world?

The scientific literature is abundant with stories of the power of systems thinking for an increasingly complex way of life. Many are learning how to abandon the outdated practices of power over people, control, compliance, and punishment, for this way of life is losing its grip everywhere. The purpose of this book is to challenge the education sector to embrace what is working all around us and consider the opportunities of this moment in time.

As a group, we concluded that our work in promoting systems thinking as a way of staying in touch with the times is not yet finished. Until systems thinking replaces static bureaucratic systems with a compliance orientation, schooling will continue to fall further behind the rapidly changing drama of working and living today.

Our group decided to meet monthly on Zoom, calling ourselves the *Systems Thinkers Think Tank*. We reflected, shared ideas, and told stories about what we had learned over our careers about the power of thinking and leading systemically. The outline of this book gradually unfolded as we drew energy and perspective from our conversations about what we now know about leading schooling in increasingly complex times.

The book begins with a chapter on the science of systems thinking, which is grounded in quantum physics and lifts the challenge of building human energy systems for the continuous improvement journey. Contemporary ideas from quality management are offered as an alternative to compliance practices, which is systems thinking in action. The third chapter takes up the issues of power in making the transition from bureaucratic thinking to systems thinking where everyone has some form of power to participate in shaping the development journey.

The chapters that follow explore the sustainability challenges of schooling today with stories from the past, research from the present, and projections for the future. Stories from a national award-winning principal illustrate the power of systems thinking in moving a high school over time to national prominence. The sustainability of the principalship itself is raised, because of current levels of resignations and the pipeline to the principalship dwindling. Networking is featured as a promising strategy for altering the stresses and isolation of the job.

The chapter on appreciative inquiry offers a fresh perspective on how strength-based living within a school can alter the culture of a school, promoting growth and development in fresh new ways with promising results. Finally, the reader is taken to the global stage of schooling and challenged with opportunities that now exist for preparing every student, every day in school, to become a competent and caring global citizen. The global stage is the new place for every school to ensure that every student prepares for their own life opportunities sustainably.

Let us take up the challenge of realigning schooling practices and cultures to the realities of the times and to the new systemic ways that people are inventing to work within institutions and across the world. The natural journey of systems thinking leads to networking as a way of life, a key to sustainable schooling. Network thinking is the new "big idea" and offers leadership opportunity for building human energy systems and vibrant cultures that lead to sustainable schooling and sustainable living!

Chapter One

Systems Thinking and Sustainable Schooling

Foundations in Physics

Karolyn J. Snyder

The United Nations (UN) general secretary, Ban Ki-Moon, predicts that sustainable development is the central challenge of our times: "Our world is under strain, for poverty continues to plague communities and families. Climate change threatens livelihoods. Conflicts are raging. Inequalities are deepening. These crises will only worsen unless we change course" (Sachs, 2015, foreword).

In 2015 the UN created 17 Sustainable Development Goals (SDGs), which is a public investment program to promote action within each nation to address those challenges" (Sachs et al., 2021). Since the launch of the SDGs, the UN has documented a decline in progress toward the goals due to the COVID-19 pandemic, unemployment, and increased poverty rates. Altering the downward trend calls for a significant scaling-up of public investments and requires global cooperation and solidarity.

The major sustainability challenges of the world today are matched by an avalanche of innovation and breakthroughs in technology, global communications, artificial intelligence, and transformations in all sectors. When considering the challenges of sustainability, and the rapid evolution of innovations, it is not difficult to understand why education has become the top UN area for global renovation.

Education plays a vital role in both continuing to advance the quality of human life, while also solving the inequities of society and the global environmental problems. The quality of life on our planet in the future depends on the quality of relevant preparation the next generations receive in school, worldwide. Already there are countries, such as Finland, applying systems thinking to national change initiatives in education (Halinen, 2017).

From a 50-year perspective on promoting systems thinking in education, and working with educators around the world, it appears that schooling as it exists in most places today is ill equipped for preparing the next generation either to resolve the global sustainable development challenges or to advance innovations that will benefit the entire human community. Schooling as we know it is basically out of step with the rapidly emerging complexities of life.

Educators need a mind shift to transform human learning systems during the schooling years (Sachs, 2015). Schooling needs to be reimagined: to switch the school's culture from top-down contentment with compliance requirements to the celebration of growth, collaboration in decision making, and innovative advancements.

Humans have always been curious about how to improve their environment. Over the last 250 years, physicists have caused a revolution in thinking that made the great innovations of our time possible. We know now, for example, that the universe, in which we live and function, is neither static nor unchanging but rather is filled with energy that promotes continuous movement and expansion (Capra & Luisi, 2016/2018). The universe is a living system that responds to the forces of galactic energy. These new understandings about life have paved the way for a tidal wave of advancements in technology and innovations for living and working.

This chapter is about how educators can learn to THINK in bold new ways about building *a human energy system* for this new global and technological age of schooling, which is a quantum worldview of organizational development. Part 1 introduces global challenges presented by the United Nations (UN), the Organisation for Economic Co-operation and Development (OECD), UNESCO, the World Economic Forum (WEF), and the Programme for International Student Assessment (PISA), which all together provide the 21st-century benchmarks for school learning.

In Part 2, we see how quantum physics/systems thinking provokes our understanding of leadership choices for redesigning schooling. Part 3 offers a 50-year story of systems thinking in action with educators around the world who explored opportunities, with a systemic approach to school development within an emerging global age of living and schooling. Part 4 provides a framework for sustainable schooling, called building a human energy system for sustainable school development, using the atom as a metaphor.

PART 1: THE GLOBAL EDUCATION CHALLENGE

Global forces are at work like never before! Now more than ever, education has a responsibility to be in gear with 21st-century challenges and aspirations and to foster the right types of knowledge, values, and skills that will lead to sustainable and inclusive growth and peaceful living. UNESCO's former director general, Irina Bokova, issued a challenge to educators that a fundamental change is needed in the way we think about education's role in global development because it has a catalytic impact on the well-being of individuals and the future of our planet (https://news.un.org/en/story/2014/11/483212). After many decades of work to resolve global challenges, the United Nations (UN) created 17 specific Sustainability Development Goals (SDGs; Sachs, 2015). Major governments of the world have recently made new commitments to fund the 17 actionable SDGs. The UN has identified three overall initiatives to move the action forward, the first of which is to expand and transform education systems. Within the education intervention cluster, there will be an anticipated overhaul of early childhood development programs, along with the quality of teachers, school leaders, class size, and the working and learning environments.

Given recent dramatic changes in work systems, it is essential that schooling prepare youth accordingly. The World Economic Forum (WEF, 2016) advanced three clusters of 21st-century skills as a new vision for education, increasing the complexity of school learning and assessment in fundamental ways. The *first skills cluster* is the foundation knowledge capacities of literacy, numeracy, and scientific and cultural literacy, which reflects the subject-based curriculum of the 20th century.

The *second skills cluster* is essential thinking and communication competencies that include complex problem solving and critical thinking, along with creativity, and collaboration. The *third and newest skills cluster* includes essential character qualities, which include curiosity, initiative, persistence, adaptability, leadership, and social awareness.

Another world organization, the OECD, recently added a fourth basic area to the PISA exam: *Global Competence.* PISA's definition of global competence is "the capacity to examine local, global and intercultural issues, to understand and appreciate the perspectives and world views of others, to engage in open, appropriate and effective interactions with people from different cultures, and to act for the collective well-being and sustainable development" (OECD, 2018).

The aim of OECD's Education 2030 Agenda is to find answers to two questions: (1) What knowledge, skills, attitudes, and values will today's students need to shape and thrive in their world in 2030? and (2) How can instructional systems be designed to develop competence in these comprehensive sets of knowledge, skills, attitudes, and values?

Finland recently created a national curriculum reform initiative, which has become a gold standard for the world (Halinen, 2017). Every community in Finland participated in the nation's curriculum reform process. Finland's story is a great example of systems thinking in action, one that also reflects the latest challenges from the UN, UNESCO, WEF, and OECD's PISA exam.

In Finland's reform efforts, *sustainability* became the overarching focus in redefining basic education. The basic premise for the new Finish national curriculum is to promote a sustainable lifestyle for all students (Halinen, 2017). Educators around the world are now learning from Finland's example how to engage the national community in transforming school learning for this moment in history.

PART 2: LESSONS FROM PHYSICS

Schooling, in general, seems to be stuck in a 20th-century mindset. A few breakout examples of school learning pave the way for global learning: the global LOGOS competitions, the Model UN Program, the International Baccalaureate Program, Well-Being and Mindfulness initiatives, and STEM research projects and competitions. The major work on schooling redesign has yet to begin, however. The traditions of bureaucratic thinking still have deep roots in Newtonian physics, which is grounded in the idea of absolute time and space.

Let us consider more deeply the roots of Newtonian physics to understand its hold on educators' thinking today. Sir Isaac Newton was the chief architect of the 17th-century scientific world (Gleick, 2003). Reasoning led him, as it had with ancient Greeks, to the concept of *atoms* as the basic element in the universe. Newton's mission was to discover the forces of nature and a system of the world, while his creed in doing so was absolute space and absolute time.

The Newtonian worldview of schooling, with fixed performance expectations for each age group, is out of sync with the dynamic adaptive systems of multi-aged cooperative adult work units that are becoming the norm in the industry, and where invention and pilots are becoming routine. A compliance orientation to work designed for the Industrial Age is rapidly being replaced in the business world with high expectations for continuous improvement, creativity, and entrepreneurship (Capra & Luisi, 2018). People are assessed more often now on their collective performance, which leads to new products and services or to refinements.

During the 18th and early 19th centuries, physicist Alexander Von Humboldt questioned that life is absolute by wandering around the globe to study living plants and people at all elevations, seasons, and various distances from the north and south poles (Wulf, 2015). Humboldt was the first to declare that the earth is a vibrant living system that grows in relation to its external environment, its location on the planet, and its place in the universe.

By the late 19th century, physicists throughout Europe began to question the universe as absolute and fixed, which led to a powerhouse of research activity that eventually confirmed Humboldt's declaration that the universe is indeed a living system that changes continuously.

Eventually, Albert Einstein's theory of relativity emerged from the mix of scientific curiosities across Europe during the turn of the 20th century, which confirmed mathematically that space and time were not absolute features of the universe but rather, space-time was one concept, which is curved by the forces of gravity (Isaacson, 2008). Neither is space empty but is filled with energy, and as such, the universe is continuously expanding. A new way of thinking was born!

In time, Einstein created $E = MC^2$, which became the most well-known equation of all time, confirming that energy is the basic element in the universe (Bodanis, 2000) and launching the age of relativity. Einstein lifted *Energy* as the major feature of the universe for the continuation of life, which is an *energy field* (energy = mass × light, which is quanta). Schrodinger was the first to use the word "entanglement" in a letter to Einstein in 1935, describing the correlation between particles when they become entangled and then inseparable over time (Wong, 2019).

Since we now understand that schools are not machines to be run and fixed when needed, educators need fresh perspectives for exploring schools as natural living systems that grow and adapt routinely to changing conditions. The atom's structure has become recognized as the source of life itself, for energy is ignited from within the atom naturally, whenever the right conditions exist.

Consider the atom (see Figure 1.1) that features a nucleus of positively charged protons and neutrons, which is *mass*, 99.9% of the atom. The bands passing through and around the nucleus are negatively charged *electrons* that excite the mass. When the right kinds of electrons are in place, and in significant amounts, new energy emerges to excite the nucleus, which then generates an atomic reaction to connect with other atoms. The new atomic connections form different kinds of molecules and compounds (e.g., helium, copper, and lead) that generate different kinds of chemical reactions.

Herein lies the story of life and the energy for growth. It is the quality of the atom's electrons and the power of its nucleus that create connections with other atoms and together generate energy for life, growth, and action. Capra and Luisi (2018) summarize the phenomenon by suggesting that "modern physics thus pictures matter not at all as passive and inert, but as being in a

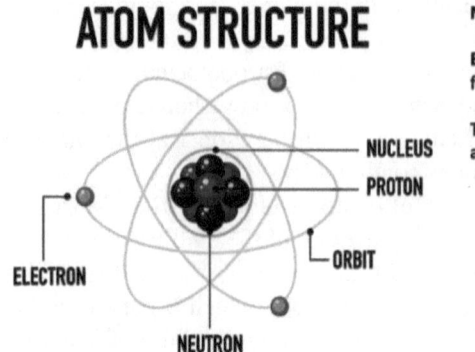

Figure 1.1. The Atom's Structure. *Adapted by Karolyn Snyder, 2022. Source: Atom Vectors by Vecteezy, https://www.vecteezy.com/free-vector/atom.*

continuous dancing and vibrating motion whose rhythmic patterns are determined by the molecular, atomic, and nuclear configurations. There is stability, but stability is one of dynamic balance" (p. 75).

Each age throughout human history has designed its own approach to educating youth. The idea that the universe is a living and dynamic system needs to be embraced to free educators to transform schools from static organizational structures with graded and subject-based curricula and prescribed learning activities. We need dynamic and energetic processes and places for learning where students are invited to be continuously curious and explore options together within and across age groups. The atom's function in generating life may enable educators to toss out the idea of absoluteness and acquire a life-affirming approach to schooling.

PART 3: LESSONS FROM A SYSTEMS THINKING INITIATIVE

Over 50 years ago a systems thinking initiative was launched that offered educators a new way of thinking about schooling: *Managing Productive Schools: Toward an Ecology* (Snyder & Anderson, 1986). Preparation for this work emerged from a series of training programs known as Managing Productive Schools (MPS; Snyder, 1988), which were offered in many places around the world. A new way of thinking about schooling was born with a foundation in systems thinking and with a new approach to practice.

Phase 1: Systems Thinking and the Interdependencies of Life around a Common Purpose

The initial spark for this systems thinking journey emerged from the pioneering work of Kast and Rosenzweig (1974): *Organization and Management: A Systems Approach* (MPS). This novel groundbreaking approach to management was a disruption to the field of business, for an organization was presented as a system that thrives on the interdependencies of all work systems around a common purpose.

Over time "quantum physics" became known as "systems thinking" in the social and behavioral sciences, which opened the floodgates for human imagination (Kast & Rosenzweig, 1974). The basic premises of Kast and Rosenzweig's new theory became the focus for our academic work, training programs, research, and publications to promote the school as a *living system* for continuous development and innovation.

Thinking from a physics perspective, systems thinking is defined here as the interrelationships and interdependencies of everything around a common purpose. It is a simple definition, yet challenging for educators who work within larger bureaucratic environments with static views of school learning, along with the relative isolation of people, structures, and programs.

Capra and Luisi (2018) argue that the major problems of our time cannot be understood in isolation from everything else, for life emerges as connected systems, such as energy, climate change, food security, water, and so forth. Systems thinking has only begun to take hold globally in the 21st century. And yet there is little evidence of systems thinking in education institutions. Consequently, there is much work ahead in preparing educators and their students for 21st-century systemic realities.

Development of Managing Productive Schools Theory

Managing productive schools training (MPS; Snyder, 1988) was designed around ten management competencies within four clusters of cooperative work: (1) organizational school goals and plans, (2) program development for learning and for resources, (3) professional development that includes training and coaching, and (4) organizational assessment of students and workers. A diagnostic tool, the School Work Culture Profile (SWCP) was designed and validated with a focus on four interdependent systems of cooperative work: school planning, professional development, curriculum development, and school assessment (Snyder et al., 2000).

This research validation study concluded that the SWCP measured one factor: the school, and its integration of four design elements around school goals (Parkinson, 1990). The SWCP has since been translated into five languages and is now being used by researchers around the world to study and improve schooling. The SWCP is also used for principal training in Sweden by Mid Sweden University (Snyder & Bjorkman, 2016). Rethinking the function of school goals and the interdependencies of programs within a collaborative work culture is making a difference in the quality of schooling for both educators and students.

In time the MPS training program became the focus of many research projects and doctoral dissertations, which yielded over 350 publications over the decades. The Pasco County School District in Florida (United States), which was the original training site for all its school leaders and district leaders, eventually became the breeding ground for many new approaches to school development. Pasco County's school success and innovation have become a Florida legend.

During the early 1990s, a group of school and district leaders from around the world, with academics, began bringing principals together annually to explore the emerging impact of global forces on school development, which eventually became known as the International School Connection (ISC; Snyder et al., 2008). A cooperative digital environment was created to promote continuous exchange and learning among members around the world (Snyder & Acker-Hocevar, 2003).

Annual global summits were held in cities such as Sochi, Tampa, Stockholm, Helsinki, Madrid, Ottawa, and Beijing for educators to visit local schools and to share, learn, and work together on the challenges of school development within the emerging global context of working and living. In time the global community of principals and academics included teachers and students with a variety of their own global learning programs and services (Snyder, 2014).

The ISC became a new kind of systems thinking initiative by linking schools together across cultures and time zones to learn about each other, as well as how global forces were impacting schooling and the integration of schools around a common purpose. Outcomes from Phase 1 of this systems thinking initiative reveal a few trends. Teaming became a central part of school life in the form of committees, task forces, study groups, partnerships, and networks (Snyder, 2015). District leaders worked with schools in new cooperative arrangements, often as interdisciplinary teams.

Students learned increasingly in cooperative teams and learning communities, engaging in team projects and competitions, even across borders (Snyder, 2014). School leaders engaged more often as partners with teachers and with parents and community groups. With the inclusion of everyone becoming responsible for shaping the school's journey, the school's culture shifted its focus to student success and well-being.

Phase 2: How Change Is Stimulated and Becomes Continuous and Sustainable

Toward the end of Phase 1 in this systems thinking initiative, we became aware of new developments in physics that were taking place at the Los Alamos National Lab to create an atom bomb using Einstein's $E = MC^2$ (Gleick, 2003). During this extraordinary and globally dangerous work, physicists observed that change over time in natural environments led to new perspectives on the change process, which became chaos theory. It appears that nothing in the universe is absolute, change is neither linear nor predictable, and all is relative depending on changing conditions.

Early systems theorists believed that a steady state of equilibrium was the desired state for growth (Capra, 1994). Chaos theory physicists found that equilibrium is a state close to death, for not much energy exists therein. It turns out that disequilibrium creates a condition that is far from equilibrium, which becomes a great energy stimulator for sustainable change (Gleick, 1987). It appears that both disequilibrium and equilibrium are central to continuous growth over time in any kind of natural system.

A few decades later the groundbreaking work of Deming (1986) and Juran (1988) emerged in Japan, called Total Quality Management (TQM), which focused on continuous improvement using statistical methods to identify reliable information for moving ahead. TQM thrives around the world today, with new emphasis given to leaders driving change. TQM uses systems thinking as a framework for decisions; creating the interdependence of functions, programs, and services; strategic planning; continuous training; and a culture of collaboration while engaging in continuous data analysis of system performance (Snyder & Snyder, 2021a).

The big ideas of chaos theory and quality management were integrated into a new publication for Phase 2 of this initiative: *Living on the Edge of Chaos: Leading Schools into the Global Age* (Snyder et al., 2000). For schools, the basic ideas of chaos theory centered on examining information that causes disruptions, followed by strategies for improvement. Energy is built for responding to the disruption by forming work groups, and then through processes of self-organization producing responsive new systems.

This natural cycle of change helps educators learn to live "on the edge of chaos" with confidence and comfort. The basic principles of systems thinking (integration of everything around a common purpose) and chaos theory (change evolves in complex and unpredictable patterns) were combined for this continuing journey of school development with a systems thinking mindset.

In March 2006, Pasco County School District leaders requested an update of the MPS training program for the digital and global age of living and

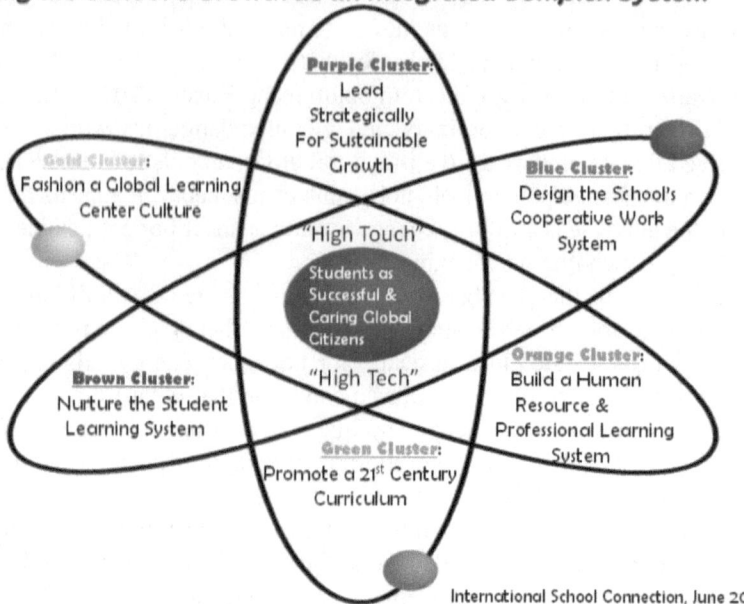

Figure 1.2. Sustainable Schooling for a Global Age. *Karolyn Snyder, International School Connection, 2017.*

schooling, which led to a 10-day training series called Leadership for Sustainable School Development (LSSD; Snyder et al., 2008) that was designed around an atomic model (see Figure 1.2). Over 12 additional authors contributed their work to the LSSD training program.

A new diagnostic tool was created, tested, and validated; it was called the Educational Quality Benchmark System (EQBS; Acker-Hocevar, 1994; Snyder, 1997). In our research on schools, we found that schools with high-quality management scores also had the highest levels of student academic performance, when ruling out socioeconomic factors. Low-quality management schools had the lowest levels of student academic success, as measured for both groups on state achievement tests (Bruner, 1997).

It is evident that leadership thinking from a quality management, systems thinking, and chaos theory perspective was impacting school performance. The new leadership anchors include the power of connections, addressing disequilibrium, building natural communication systems, celebrating complex adaptive systems, acting on information, and possessing an intention to improve the quality of life.

In time it became clear that leadership thinking is the most vital factor in success with a systems approach to schooling. The big ideas that have evolved in physics over the last 100 years have become useful guideposts and anchors for thinking about how to move schooling from a machine metaphor to one of schools as living systems. School leaders begin to relax while realizing the power of the big ideas from physics, and the seeming miracles that evolve from a more natural orientation to schooling.

PART 4: BUILDING A HUMAN ENERGY SYSTEM FOR SUSTAINABLE SCHOOLING

A primary challenge for educators today in redesigning schooling is to build a human energy system for development within a school while also working within larger bureaucratic institutions. Building a human energy system for sustainable schooling (see Figure 1.3) is a metaphor for the atom and a mindset for strategically and intentionally developing sustainable schooling.

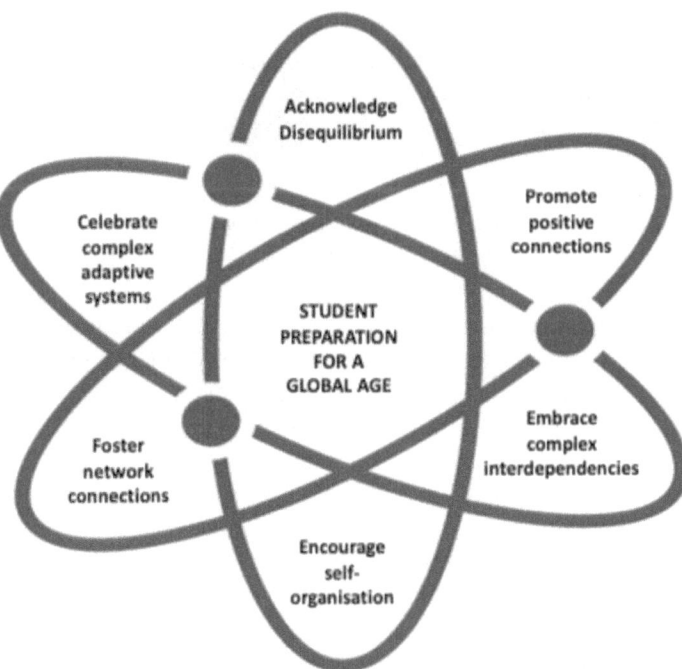

Figure 1.3. Building a Human Energy System for Sustainable Schooling. *Karolyn Snyder, 2022. Source: Atom Vectors by Vecteezy, https://www.vecteezy.com/free-vector/atom.*

Sustainability is defined here as the adequate responsiveness of a natural system to changes in the environment.

In essence, the human energy system is a systemic example of what scientists are calling *quantum entanglement* (Wong, 2019), which is a state in which a system can only be expressed in terms of its sum effects. Individual particles, such as employees in an organization, become entangled to produce impressive outcomes. Let us now consider the sub-particles, or electrons, that are features of the human energy system, which together and entangled generate high energy systems.

The nucleus of the atom in this metaphor is student preparation for living and working in a global age. Consider the following metaphoric electronic bands, which are big ideas in physics today. These ideas are the new habits of mind for leading the school transformation journey. The quality of the six big ideas needs to be sufficiently strong so that enough energy is generated for a school's life-affirming journey of nurturing student development for a global age of living.

Electronic Band 1: Disequilibrium That Is Acknowledged Leads to Self-Organization

Scientists tell us that systems far from equilibrium, in a state of disequilibrium, naturally possess a dynamic of self-renewal. The edge of chaos exists somewhere between stability and turbulence and is the place where a complex system is the most spontaneous, adaptive, and creative. Disequilibrium prompts new kinds of collective action and novel resolutions.

Consider the challenges of the COVID-19 pandemic worldwide. Schooling became instantly virtual, or nothing at all, and we now understand that a school's capacity to adapt to the new reality varied widely across communities, nations, and regions of the world (Snyder & Snyder, 2021a). Where teaming was the norm in schools, and where digital cultures were complex and creative, useful adaptations were made to teaching and learning. Leadership thinking made all the difference in how resources were made available and how well teachers were prepared for using virtual and hybrid solutions (Snyder et al., 2021).

The emergence of a new order of schooling is a gradual process that lives between disequilibrium and self-organization and is also filled with surprise. Order and stability emerge from within a complex system as it adapts to new conditions. To be clear, natural growth is irregular, random, discontinuous, erratic, complex, and yet stable. Information is the primary source of disequilibrium, which is also the lifeline to a sustainable future. The disorder can become the new order, for life is an emergent phenomenon that thrives at the edge of chaos.

Electronic Band 2: Positive Connections Lead to Interconnectivity and Networking

A basic law of physics is that where there are no connections, there is no energy for growth. Where there are minimal connections, as in teaching teams, there is modest energy, and where there are teaching teams, plus simultaneous school-wide work units, partnerships, and networks, a school generates its own energy system, which is a natural phenomenon.

Connections are the central feature in the story of life and its energy for the future. Another basic law of physics is that negative energy builds negatively and must be stopped or decline is predictable. Positive energy, however, builds positively, leading to desired outcomes. We see evidence of this in the various movements toward "mindfulness" and "well-being" for students and teachers when used routinely. Positive energy leads to life-affirming learning environments.

When entering a school, within a few minutes its energy system becomes apparent. Where there is silence, there is virtually no energy exhibited for exploring and learning about the world and how it works. Where clusters of students and teachers engage in projects together, with an operational accountability system, chatter is abundant about knowledge, exploration activity, and the new ideas that naturally evolve. The energy system of a school tells its own story about the quality of life for teachers and students and its potential sustainability.

Human networking is a rather new idea for schools (Snyder & Snyder, 2021b). Rather than being designed intentionally, networks emerge naturally once the idea "it takes all of us" is realized. It can be predicted that *network thinking* will in time become a new norm for high-performing schools. Scientists observe that networks create their own energy system and expand as interests and needs emerge (Buchanan, 2002).

"Multiple leaders" is a major characteristic of networks, where power comes from the unifying purpose and a specific function that advances the organization. A surprising find is this: The more complex the network, the fewer fluctuations there are in its performance and growth. The most stable type of network is complex.

Electronic Band 3: Complexity Leads to Complex Adaptive Systems

Few can argue that life has become increasingly complex on every scale and in every context. Physicists tell us that complexity is a natural feature of growing and thriving systems, and complexity grows in complex ways (Snyder et al., 2008). Complex systems cannot be controlled; however, they can be influenced in certain directions.

Quantum entanglement occurs when employees, programs, services, partnerships, and networks are linked together so strongly that the effect is powerful and results from strong connections. *Entanglement* is the new big idea for generating energy in a school or school district that propels schooling forward sustainably into the current dynamics of our rapidly changing world.

A few high-performing schools have become lighthouses for new approaches to school learning, where continuous feedback and information are the lifeblood of the organization. Complex adaptive schools thrive in the space between what is known and what needs to be known and achieved. This organic approach to leading schools embraces disruption, builds new alliances and networks to address emerging disturbances, encourages novelty and surprise, promotes multiple options for addressing challenges, and supports networking as a way of life.

CONCLUSION AND CALL TO ACTION

It is time to activate our curiosity and explore possibilities for shaping sustainable and adaptable systems of schooling for the 21st century. In time, new confidence emerges with the successful and continuous use of the metaphor: building a human energy system. This challenge is the educator's opportunity to make a profound and long-lasting difference!

Consider how school programs and services might become more tightly integrated and entangled around the common purpose of student preparation for success in this global age of living. How might the challenges of disequilibrium be addressed more fearlessly to propel growth forward? And how might the energy-building electronic bands be strengthened? And finally, how might teams, task forces, partnerships, and networks become stronger by becoming more entangled? These are fundamental considerations for building a human energy system for sustainable schooling.

REFERENCES

Acker-Hocevar, M. (1994). *The content validation of standards, outcomes, and indicators of organizational development in region IV of Florida*. Dissertation. University of South Florida, Tampa.

Bodanis, D. (2000). $E = mc^2$: *A biography of the world's most famous equation*. Berkley Books.

Bruner, D. (1997). *The dynamics of work cultures of low and high performing schools: A case study*. Doctoral Dissertation, University of South Florida, Tampa.

Buchanan. M. (2002). *NEXUS: Small worlds and the ground-breaking theory of networks*. W.W. Norton & Company.
Capra, F. (1994). *The Tao of physics* (3rd ed). Shambala.
Capra, F., & Luisi, P. L. (2016, 2018). *The systems view of life: A unifying vision.* Cambridge University Press.
Deming, W. E. (1986). *Out of crisis*. Massachusetts Institute of Technology.
Gleick, J. (1987). *Chaos: Making a new science*. Penguin Books.
Gleick, J. (2003). *Isaac Newton*. Random House, Inc.
Halinen I. (2017). *The conceptualization of competencies related to sustainable development and sustainable lifestyles.* Paris: UNESCO, International Bureau of education series, current and critical issues in curriculum, learning and assessment.
Isaacson, W. (2008). *Einstein: The man, the genius, and the theory of relativity*. Andre Deutsch, The Carlton Publishing Group.
Juran, J. M. (1988). *Juran on planning for quality*. The Free Press.
Kast, F., & Rosenzweig, J. (1974). *Organizational management: A systems approach*. McGraw-Hill, Inc.
OECD. (2018). *PISA 2018 Global Competence*. http://www.oecd.org/pisa/pisa-2018-global-competence.htm
Parkinson. A. (1990). *An examination of the reliability and factor structure of the School Work Culture Profile*. Doctoral dissertation. University of South Florida, Tampa.
Sachs, J. D. (2015). *The age of sustainable development*. Columbia University Press.
Sachs, J. D., Kroll, C., Lafortune, G., Fuller, G., & Finn, W. (2021). *Sustainable development report 2021: The decade of action for sustainable development goals*. Cambridge University Press.
Snyder, K. J. (1988). *Competency development for managing productive schools*. Harcourt, Brace & Jovanovich.
Snyder, K. J. (2019). Preparing globally competent students: The K-12 schooling challenge. In W. B. James & C. Cobanoglu (Eds.), *Advances in Global Education and Research, 3*, 136–149.
Snyder, K. J., Acker-Hocevar, M., & Snyder, K. M. (2000, 2008), *Living on the edge of chaos: Leading schools into the global age*. ASQ The Quality Press.
Snyder, K. J., & Anderson, R. H. (1986). *Managing productive schools: Toward an ecology*. Harcourt, Brace & Jovanovich.
Snyder, K. J., Mann, J., Johnson, E., & Xing, M. (2010). Connecting schools across borders: A global partnership. *Innovation Magazine*, Fall, 5–13.
Snyder, K. J., & Snyder, K. M. (2021a). Building sustainable systems of schooling in turbulent times. In J. Glanz (Ed.), *Crisis and pandemic leadership: Implications for meeting the needs of students, teachers, and parents*. Roman & Littlefield.
Snyder, K. J., & Snyder, K. M. (2021b). The human networked organization: Toward contemporary quality management and sustainability. Paper presentation at the 27th International Sustainable Development Research Society Conference, Östersund. November 8–10.

Snyder, K. M. (1997). *A construct validation and reliability estimation of the educational quality benchmark system.* Doctoral dissertation. University of South Florida, Tampa.

Snyder, K. M. (2014). Concept mapping, voice thread, visual images: Helping teachers spawn divergent thinking and dialogic learning. In L. Shedletsky & J. Beaudry (Eds.), *Cases on teaching and critical thinking through visual representation strategies.* IGI Global Publishers.

Snyder, K. M. (2015). Engaged leaders develop schools as quality organizations. *International Journal of Quality and Service Sciences, 7* (2/3), 217–229.

Snyder, K. M., & Acker-Hocevar, M. (2003). Building international cultures of synergy through online social networks. In F. Kochran (Ed.), *International perspective on mentoring.* Information Age Press.

Snyder, K. M., & Bjorkman, C. (2016). Systematisk skol- och kvalitetsutveckling med SWCP School Work Culture Profile. In F. Sundh & U. Auno (Eds.), *Methodhandbok for forskolechefer och rektorer.* Studentlitteratur AB.

Snyder, K. M., Johnson, M., & Snyder, K. J. (2021). Going hybrid on a dime: Lessons from schooling during the pandemic and implications for sustainable quality in education. Paper presented at the 14th Annual International Conference on Education, Research and Innovation, Sevilla, Spain November 8–10, 2021.

Snyder, K. M., & Snyder, K. J. (1996). Developing integrated work cultures: Findings from a study of school change. *NASSP Bulletin,* 80 (576) January.

Wong, B. (2019). On quantum entanglement. *International Journal of Automatic Control System, 5*(2), 1–7.

World Economic Forum. (2016). Ten 21st century skills every student needs. https://www.weforum.org/agenda/2016/03/21st-century-skills-future-jobs-students/

Wulf, A. (2015). *The invention of nature: Alexander von Humboldt's new world.* Vintage Books.

Chapter Two

Expanding How We Think about Quality in Education

Kristen M. Snyder

The quality movement in education is currently dominated by political accountability programming at the expense of teaching and learning (Ravitch, 2010). The heavy emphasis on high-stakes testing under the auspices of accountability has dominated, replacing learning with competition. Studies demonstrate what educators have known for years: the politics of education, with a focus on accountability, is counterproductive if schools are going to meet the global imperative for a sustainable society.

Many educators and researchers argue that it is time to rethink what is meant by quality in education and how to prepare school leaders for the job if education will be sustainable. This plea comes at a time when education has been singled out by UNESCO as essential to achieving sustainable development, articulating a new agenda to "reorient education to help people develop knowledge, skills, values, and behaviors needed for sustainable development" (UNESCO, 2017).

The ability of an organization to adapt quickly to customer needs at all levels is a contemporary indicator of quality (Deleryd & Fundin, 2020; Tinsley et al., 2021). Creating organizational infrastructures that are fluid and flexible, while at the same time grounded in the organization's values and customer needs, is paramount if business and organizations in society will succeed as an actor in the UN 2030 Agenda on Sustainable Development.

To truly connect sustainability and quality management requires that organizations adopt values that reflect a care for society and the planet, which are promoted by the organization's fundamental practices. The values are drivers that keep adaptation in line with future goals. To merely change the structure, without being grounded in a set of values, places organizations at risk of failure (Mårtensson et al., 2019).

Researchers in quality management suggest there is a paradigm conflict between current organizational forms and what is needed for meeting the complex demands of society today (Van Kemenade & Hardjono, 2019). One of the biggest challenges for leaders today is how to "position and enable organizations and people for adaptability in the face of increasingly dynamic and demanding environments" (Uhl-Bien & Arena, 2018, p. 1). A different kind of organizational infrastructure is called for that promotes adaptability and responsiveness (Suarez & Montes, 2020) and a new mindset (Rill, 2016).

The purpose of this chapter is to reexamine the concept of quality in education from a contemporary quality management perspective. Since the 1990s, quality management has expanded to embrace the principles of chaos and complexity theory, which provides new insights into leading in an age of complexity. This expanded perspective is important for educators to develop and sustain quality in schools to prepare youth with knowledge and skills for living and working in the future.

The chapter is divided into five sections. Part 1 provides a historical review of quality in education. Part 2 presents contemporary perspectives from quality management, which serve as a rationale for a mind shift. In Part 3, the need for a mind shift is further explored from a leadership perspective. Part 4 presents the chaos theory of change model, and in Part 5 a case study is presented to illustrate sustainable quality development that is based on this mindset.

PART 1: QUALITY IN EDUCATION: A HISTORICAL OVERVIEW

The 1990s witnessed a new language in education with a focus on quality management that spread across Europe and the North American continents. The sun was shining with the promise that educators would be supported with resources and processes to inject a systematic approach to continuous improvement that could help educators ensure students would be prepared for a future workforce. The "new promised land" was based on a business excellence model from total quality management (Deming, 1986).

Quality management provided leaders with a systematic approach to designing products and services to meet the needs of the customers. "Educators, get on board because quality management is the new way to measure school success." Program initiatives in Europe were spearheaded under titles such as *Schools and Quality* (OECD, 1992), *Measuring the Quality of Schools* (OECD, 1995), and *Performance Standards in Education: In Search of Quality* (OECD, 1995).

In the United States, the Malcolm Baldridge Award was adapted for schools and new measures such as the Education Quality Benchmark System (Snyder et al., 2000) were designed. These frameworks integrated the principles of quality management and systems thinking to serve as a navigational tool to continuously monitor and adapt school practices to meet customer needs.

It didn't take many years before the bubble of sunshine burst in the United States and later in England and other parts of Europe. Educational policy quickly shifted from a paradigm of systematic continuous improvement to one of accountability. A systems view of continuous quality improvement was replaced by standardized measures and international comparisons, such as IEA Reading Literacy, TIMSS, PISA, and PIRLS (Snyder, 2007).

More than three decades later, numerous studies demonstrated that the heavy emphasis on high-stakes testing has been devastating for schools and youth in many countries (Westling Allodi, 2013). Rather than creating spaces of learning, educators changed their teaching to ensure that students would score high on achievement tests. In effect, assessment criteria defined the curricula in many schools, shaped the learning activities, and ultimately determined what knowledge is. If schools are to be sustainable, the very notion of quality and the mechanisms with which quality is achieved and measured need to be revisited.

Many argue that defining quality in education needs to consider an expanded view that includes not only outcomes of youth, but also the organizational environment and experiences that are created to stimulate learning. Sustaining quality requires that we recognize the dynamic nature of schooling that is influenced by changes in society, including technology, socioeconomic factors, and cultural and political environments. In his view, evolutions in the workforce and society will necessarily alter what, and how schools, develop their internal systems of teaching and learning, suggesting that quality is a dynamic process.

Murgatroyd and Morgan (1994) suggested there are two primary models for defining quality in education: quality assurance and quality improvement. Accordingly, "quality assurance refers to the determination of standards, appropriate methods and quality requirements by an expert body, accompanied by a process of inspection or evaluation that examines the extent to which practice meets these standards" (p. 45). This view is based on a competitive model, driven by governmental frameworks, audits, and inspections.

Quality improvement is customer oriented and focused on an internal locus of control that is guided by members of the organization. This approach is in line with the tenets of total quality management (TQM), which is characterized by five main principles: (1) management commitment, (2) focus on the customer and the employee, (3) focus on facts, (4) continuous improvement, and (5) everybody's participation (Murgatroyd & Morgan, 1994). Services and products are designed and improved with the customer in mind and often include customers in the development process. Leaders are seen as facilitators of growth rather than as autocratic managers.

PART 2: QUALITY MANAGEMENT IN THE 21ST CENTURY: INTEGRATING SUSTAINABILITY

In the field of quality management today, new questions are considered about what quality in an age of sustainability and global competitiveness is. The historical development of quality has witnessed four major eras, each with its own vision and definition, reflecting and evolving from inspection and control to total quality management that gained strength in the 1980s. Current research in quality management suggests that we are now in a new era, Quality 5.0, in which sustainability is a key component, expanding the notion of the customer (Deleryd & Fundin, 2020).

Ramanathan (2021) argues that the traditional models of quality that are based on economic indicators and performance measures are far too limited. Among other things, the definition of quality needs to include society as a customer. If quality is, among other things, satisfying customer needs, and we are to meet and satisfy global sustainable development goals, then society is necessarily a part of the quality equation (Deleryd & Fundin, 2020).

In other studies, quality is described in terms of paradigms. Van Kemenade and Hardjono (2019) identified them as (1) the *empirical paradigm*: quality is conformance to requirements; (2) the *reference paradigm*: quality is fitness for use; and (3) the *reflective paradigm*: quality is subjective. They conclude that we are now entering a fourth paradigm, the *emergent paradigm*, which builds on systems thinking, self-organizing principles, and relates to complex adaptive systems. "The emergence paradigm defines quality in a dialogue of all stakeholders . . . knowing quality can be different tomorrow" (p. 160).

Quality is seen as dynamic, not static, based on shared values, flexible, adaptable, dialog and communication-oriented, participatory, shared leadership, strategic, and systems-oriented (Van Kemenade & Hardjono, 2019). If our knowledge and understanding about quality is shifting to reflect the paradigm of emergence, self-organization, out-of-the-box thinking, participatory practice, and sustainability among other things, what implications does this have for leading schools?

Advances in the field of quality management also recognize that quality is more than just tools, processes, and outcome measures (Park-Dahlgaard

& Dahlgaard, 2003). Repeated failures in quality management initiatives (no matter the industry) were explained by a lack of focus on organizational culture as a key component to achieving quality (Snyder et al., 2018). Performance measurement systems (PMS) serve well as a tool to quantify effectiveness and efficiency in organizational practice; however, they often lack a focus on the human culture dimension.

Park-Dahlgaard and Dahlgaard (2003) argue that quality management systems need to integrate the human dimension. Developing and sustaining quality requires that leaders care about their number one asset: people. In their definition of quality, they propose leaders focus on the four Ps: people, partnership, processes of work, and products/service development. These become the preconditions necessary to sustain quality in organizations.

Similarly, Shingo Institute (2017) designed another model for quality that reinforces the human dimension within an organization. According to Dr. Shingo, "tools and systems alone do not operate a business. People do" (2017, p. 11). The Shingo model contains five interdependent components that create the conditions for quality: results, tools, culture, systems, and guiding principles. The guiding principles are central to the success of sustainable quality management, which reflects a developing awareness of the importance of concretizing the dialog on culture and values within systems for business excellence.

PART 3: SUSTAINING QUALITY IN EDUCATION: THE NEED FOR A MIND SHIFT

The global imperative to address sustainable development is pressing organizational leaders to reexamine internal practices to align systems of work with values that promote sustainable development (Hawkins & James, 2018). New organizational systems need to be grounded for building healthy work environments to meet customer needs and invite innovation. With the growing recognition that society is now considered a customer, the internal work systems, routines, and practices will necessarily need to integrate and link with sustainable societal development goals (Mårtensson et al., 2019).

Creating the conditions for organizational transformation within complex systems may require leaders to think beyond the box. Achieving this mind shift will require leaders to move from linear/static thinking to random/dynamic thinking, in which functions are seen as interrelated and systemic. This has implications for organizational structure and the culture. Suarez and Montes (2020) hypothesize that building organizational resilience requires organizational routines and simple rules, which combined with improvisation are the key ingredients for resilience, suggesting the balance between structure and culture is paramount.

Snyder et al. (2018) found that many organizational leaders struggle to understand how to balance structure with culture to create the conditions to sustain quality in an age of complexity. All too often, the focus is given to structure and policy, ignoring the power and importance of people, with their values, and behaviors as key ingredients for sustainable organizational development. They also found that leaders who understand the importance of connecting structure and culture have stronger internal systems that are adaptive and responsive to change.

Of interest is to explore what knowledge leaders need to break the rules, while remaining accountable. Insights are offered from chaos and complexity theory, as well as systems theory. Systems thinking can alter how we think about change and building sustainable school programs and services (Shaked & Schechter, 2017), while chaos and complexity theory helps us to understand adaptability and resilience. Developing an understanding of these theories and their application in organizations provides leaders with tools for a necessary mind shift toward sustainable quality development in schools.

PART 4: THE CHAOS THEORY OF CHANGE

Over the last five decades, our collective work with schools and educational leaders has focused on the school as a living dynamic system with the integration of work functions around the core purpose of student success for sustainable futures (Snyder et al., 2008). Quality practices become strategies for addressing the changing and complex needs of students, communities, and society.

Drawing on insights from the sciences, the chaos theory of change model (Snyder et al., 2008) was envisioned to help leaders develop a systems approach to leading sustainable quality in schools. The model is in line with the principles found in Quality 5.0 and the emergence paradigm (Fundin et al., 2021), which integrates sustainable development as part of quality management.

The chaos theory of change (Snyder et al., 2008) addresses the dynamic of change over time, which is based on theoretical principles from *system thinking* (Capra & Luisi, 2016), *chaos and complexity theories* (Kaufman, 1995), and *networking science* (Barabasi, 2003). A systems view of life creates the mindset that everyone is working together toward a common purpose. It reflects a shift toward a multidisciplinary strategy for development that is

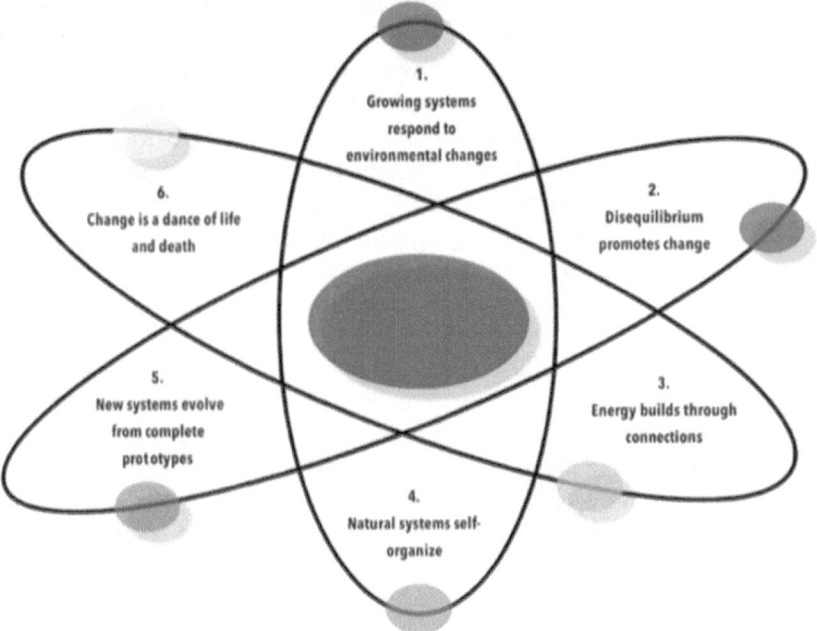

Figure 2.1. Chaos Theory of Change. *Snyder et al., 2008.*

relationship oriented, embraces mapping possibilities rather than evaluation systems, and measures success in quality, values, and process.

Systems thinking naturally leads to greater complexity, which strengthens a system's cohesiveness and resilience. Surprise becomes routine within a system with a nonlinear set of rules, with energy systems of cohesive connections (Snyder & Snyder, 2021). A dynamic network of many agents works in parallel, constantly acting and reacting to what other agents are doing and learning. Control is decentralized as agents continuously learn from each other and the environment about change and possibilities.

The chaos theory of change (Figure 2.1) includes six main stages: (1) growing systems respond to environmental changes, (2) disequilibrium promotes change, (3) energy builds through connections, (4) natural systems self-organize, (5) new systems evolve from complete prototypes, and (6) change is a dance of life and death.

The first lesson suggests that external forces impact human organizations and only increase over time in their complexity. The leadership function is to acknowledge both internal and external paradoxes and to become an influence on the external environment as well as the organization's responses to changing conditions. The second lesson suggests that disequilibrium, rather than stability, stimulates the system to respond in the most dynamic, fundamental, and sustainable ways. The leadership task is to use the information to stimulate disequilibrium, which provides the energy and focus for change.

From the third lesson we understand that the stronger the web of interactions, the stronger the forces and human energy for change. The leadership function is to develop professional capacities, partnerships, and networks to respond to emerging challenges in the system. The fourth lesson teaches us that natural systems have a strong capacity to respond to both external and internal forces, to self-organize, and to become self-determining. The leadership function is to respond to and develop the organization's internal readiness to adapt to changing conditions.

In the fifth lesson, we understand that building prototypes eventually leads to total systems that are composed of multiples of those prototypes. The leadership task is to sponsor the development of completely new forms; the system of services and practices is transformed. In the sixth, and final lesson, we learn that the process of creation and destruction is the cosmic dance in natural systems, whereby energy patterns are dissolved and rearranged to fit emerging conditions.

Based on this model, the leadership task is to promote both the end and the beginning of work systems, structures, and services. For sustainability to continue, there needs to be a balance between disorganized and organized complexity, where variations no longer cancel one another out, but rather become reinforcing.

In complex adaptive systems, the following characteristics are found naturally: a variety of networks, continuous interactions, self-organizing, interconnections, emergence, dynamics, and coevolution. Some leaders identify sustainability strategies and begin to map sustainability issues while working with cross-divisional teams, outside consultants, and external stakeholders. Leaders shift their roles during a transition from a directive role to one of support and mentoring. Building an agile enterprise means finding the right balance between standardizing operations and pursuing innovation.

As Suarez and Montes (2020) point out, adaptability also requires routine and structure; it is in the balance between the two that complexity can thrive and serve as a catalyst for innovation and change. Understanding complex adaptive systems is part of the equation of quality in education. To reorient education toward sustainable development in part means developing adaptive environments within schools that are based on networks, teaming, and systems thinking, in which leaders serve as mentors rather than accountability officers.

PART 5: CASE EXAMPLE

In this section of the chapter, the expanded view of quality, based on the chaos theory of change and the emergence paradigm, is illustrated using data from a five-year study of a private school in Florida (Snyder, 2019; Snyder & Snyder, 2021). Over the last 25 years, the school has evolved into a rather novel networked system of learning and living within a rapidly changing local and global context.

Continuous improvement initiatives over time have transformed the school's work systems into a network of activity both internally and externally. This alters our understanding of how collaborative systems can emerge over time into a complex network of energy that pushes the boundaries of excellence. As well, they have integrated the sustainable development goals into the school's mission and vision.

A Team-Based Organization Grounded in Values and a Systems Orientation

Corbett Preparatory School of IDS (CPS) is an independent school in Tampa, Florida (United States), with about 520 students, pre-K through middle school, which recently celebrated its 50th anniversary. Members of the student body and teaching faculty are international, bringing global perspectives naturally to school learning. The professional staff and students are organized into learning communities, with many additional special programs that are offered during the school day, evenings, weekends, and summers to accelerate learning.

The curriculum is guided by the International Baccalaureate Program, the *More Options for Results in Education Program (M.O.R.E. Approach)* (Cohen, 2003), and the International School Connection Global Learning Center Benchmarks, which integrate the UN sustainability goals with core curricula and pedagogical practice. The M.O.R.E. Approach is a continuous improvement model developed over a 25-year period. The approach reflects a variety of theoretical, practical, and value-based practices to support pedagogical development and a culture for social and emotional well-being.

The school's leadership is based on systems thinking, quality management, and chaos theory as conceptual guideposts to support organizational sustainability, continuous improvement, and customer satisfaction. Characteristic of the school is the continuous development of new approaches to learning and organization that drive professional development and a culture of continuous learning and improvement.

Teachers assume responsibility beyond their primary jobs for initiatives across the school, forming a vast network of interconnectivity that raises the level of performance significantly for adults and students. The professional staff participates weekly in workshops at the school, while small groups and individuals also participate in a variety of other programs to advance their own knowledge and to then strengthen the school's performance. State, national, and international student, staff, and team awards are common, as is the recognition of the school as a unit.

In this purpose-driven organization, workers take on new chores and challenges in response to the emerging demands of the growing system. The phenomenon is clearly a network of growing clusters of initiatives, with new kinds of leadership roles emerging, and where human energy is a force for innovation. The network emerged naturally over time as the professional staff pursued ideas for enriching the learning environment for its students. The school leader's role also shifted from supervising individuals to managing the systems of work and the health of the school's culture and its impact on every learner.

Teachers are responsible for everything that occurs within their learning communities while mentoring and coaching each other to "Olympic" performance. Professional dialogue is a dominant feature, which spills over into the daily life of work with students. New teachers are trained in every core program of value to the school prior to their teaching debut. The administrative teams appear to have one purpose, and that is to support the work of teachers in achieving high success levels for each student.

Think Outside the Box

During the COVID-19 pandemic crisis, the school demonstrated a different approach to sustainable quality development that was in line with Quality 5.0 and the emergence paradigm. Illustrated below are five key factors that were observed: (1) think outside the box and break the rules; (2) move from linear thinking to random thinking; (3) embrace a systems orientation; (4) combine routines and rules with improvisation; and (5) encourage networking among workers.

After three months of virtual teaching and learning during the initial stages of the pandemic, the school leaders recognized the need for a long-term solution that would support health and learning, and also maintain the school's values. The plan for reopening the school was to offer a hybrid model in which teaching teams would carry out their classes with both remote learners and classroom-based learners simultaneously. To arrange this approach, required changes in the on-site school facilities, ongoing professional development (PD) for teachers, and rethinking of the way technology were used in the classroom.

The plan was crystallized in two strategic plans, which provided the framework for new solutions. In the remote learning plan, the goals are clearly stated, "to provide opportunities for our children to be engaged in learning in the absence of being here on our beautiful campus." As well, the plan asked teachers to think outside of the box and provide opportunities for students to read, write, share ideas, explore, create, play, and move (so as not to stagnate in front of a screen).

For the students, they were #ONECOMMUNITY despite connections using technology. Classroom and remote learners were paired in dialogue groups to complete assignments. In science classes, remote learners served as process observers for in-class experiments and Zoom breakout rooms that connect students in dialogue about group assignments. Scheduling was flipped upside down, as were the patterns of mobility between classrooms to ensure safety.

Moving from Linear Thinking to Random Thinking

As part of the "one community" culture, it was important to keep connections strong with remote learners and to boost morale as a critical component of well-being. Teachers designed small events such as "Operation curbside pick-me-up" to stay connected. They drove to student homes in cars decorated with banners that read "We love you," and greeted the remote students at their doorsteps giving them "high-fives," safely with the help of a wooden hand. As the teachers shared on the school's Facebook page, "It was an uplifting way to spend an afternoon for all involved."

Feedback Loops

Open lines of communication were vital for the school to keep its finger on the pulse during the pandemic. The leadership team conducted regular feedback from parents and teachers throughout the implementation phases to ensure continuous quality. The data collected enabled the school to adjust its policies and procedures throughout the year. At the start of the school year, the teachers welcomed 64% (323) of its enrolled students on campus and 36% (178) remotely via Zoom. By the end of the school year, 91% of students were on campus while only 9% remained remote.

Embrace a Systems Orientation

At CPS, team teaching and cooperative learning are the foundations for developing responsive learning systems. The hybrid model provided new opportunities for team teaching in a variety of ways, including scheduling and flexibility to better meet the needs of students. The integration of the arts in general education stimulated new insights and dialogue about partnering to co-design the curriculum.

Combine Routines and Rules with Improvisation

Improvisation became a norm at the school as educators sought creative ways to combine the values of the school with the practical needs of students and the community. Throughout the year they held drive-through awards ceremonies that were created to reinforce the value of students and maintain safety for individuals and the community.

Encourage Networking among Workers

As part of the learning community, parents were also seen as part of the network of learning. "The Corbett Prep Family Remote Learning Plan: A Guide to Continuing Learning from Home, the Remote Learning Plan" communicated to parents the school's intent to design innovative solutions that were grounded in the values and principles of the school. As expressed on the first page of the plan,

> We all understand that the face-to-face interactions in the vibrant and engaging classrooms our students and teachers enjoy each day are better in-person than occurring remotely. However, what we seek to create is a remote learning environment where teachers and students continue to be engaged in ways made possible by our many options for learning via the connectedness of the internet. There are many alternative and effective approaches available to our teachers to keep our student's minds active in meaningful ways. But parents, we need your help. (p. 1)

Student Success and Well-Being

Considering questions of quality, it is perhaps also of interest to understand the degree to which the school's approach to adaptability and resilience contributed to learning and employee well-being. Each year student test scores are recorded on the national Measure of Academic Progress (MAP) using the RIT (Rasch Unit) scale to help teachers measure and compare academic growth (Snyder et al., 2021). Comparative data from 2019 to 2020 showed that almost all grade levels exhibit the same or higher mean RIT scores.

Employee well-being also remained strong during the pandemic, a result that was most unexpected given the strains on educators to deliver quality education during a crisis. Well-being data were collected annually as part of the Contentment Foundation project with Yale University, recording strength among staff despite the pandemic. The Well-Being Survey collects data on physical health, psychological well-being, community climate, inner climate, relationship to experiences, and emotional efficacy. Corbett Prep has been conducting these surveys since its inception in June 2019.

In August 2020, Corbett Prep began arguably the toughest year of teaching in the school's history. Managing student engagement online and in person, amidst a pandemic, was challenging for everyone. As the school entered the 2021–2022 school year, the faculty and staff recorded their highest ever overall well-being score of 72.49. These findings for both academic success and well-being are strong indicators of a quality work culture that enabled the educators to adapt and sustain quality despite the pandemic.

This case example illustrates how achieving and sustaining quality require highly developed systems and infrastructure that are adaptative and resilient. Present also are clearly articulated values and principles that serve to anchor decisions amidst the chaos. Understanding the fluid nature of living systems that is reflected in chaos, complexity, and systems theories, provided a framework necessary for the leaders to achieve a mind shift to reorient their school to sustain quality through adaptability. When leaders combine big ideas from the sciences with established quality management practices, innovation emerges.

CALL TO ACTION

Creating conditions for sustainable quality development that includes societal sustainable development requires a mind shift that builds on systems thinking, values human interaction, and keeps alive sustainability as part of the broader value-based mission and vision. Achieving organizational success is well served when strategic leaders build cultures of trust and commitment that motivate people to become engaged and create conditions for sustainable quality development. This only happens in a living community of people who are passionate about the mission and about each other on the journey.

Key ideas in strategic thinking require keeping your eye on the big idea, keeping your ears to the ground and your eyes and senses alert for changing winds. Leaders who build energy systems of all kinds nurture this dance of "Life at the Edge of Chaos," which is part of the equation to connecting quality management and sustainable societal development. Educators, the choice is yours—to succumb to the limitations of accountability or to develop a systems orientation to quality in schools in which accountability measures become but one part of the indicator of success.

REFERENCES

Barabasi, A-L. (2003). *Linked: How everything is connected to everything else and what it means for business, science, and everyday life.* PLUME Penguin Group.

Capra, F., & Luisi, P. L. (2016/2018). *The systems view of life: A unifying vision.* Cambridge University Press.

Cohen, D. (2003). *It's all about the kids: Every child deserves a "Teacher of the Year."* Bee Happy Publishing.

Deleryd, M., & Fundin, A. (2020). Towards societal satisfaction in a fifth generation of quality: The sustainability model. *Total Quality Management & Business Excellence*, 1–17.

Deming, E. (1986). *Out of crisis.* MIT Center for Advanced Engineering Study.

Fundin, A., Backström, T., & Johansson, P. E. (2021). Exploring the emergent quality management paradigm. *Total Quality Management & Business Excellence*, *32*(5–6), 476–488.

Hawkins, M. J., & James, C. (2018). Developing a perspective on schools as complex, evolving loosely linking systems. *Educational Management Administration & Leadership*, *46*(5), 729–748.

Kaufman, S. (1995). *At home in the universe: The search for laws of self-organisation and complexity.* Oxford University Press.

Mårtensson, A., Snyder, K., & Ingelsson, P. (2019). Lean and sustainability: How ready are leaders? *The TQM Journal*, *31*(2), 136–149.

Murgatroyd, S., & Morgan C. (1994). *Total quality management and the school.* Open University Press.

OECD (Organisation for Economic Co-operation and Development). (1992). *High quality education and training.* OECD.

OECD. (1995). *Measuring the quality of schools.* OECD.

OECD. (1995). *Performance standards in education: In search of quality.* OECD.

Park-Dahlgaard, S. M., & Dahlgaard, J. (2003). Human dimension: Critical to sustainable quality development. In T. Conti, Y. Kondo, & G. Watson (Eds.), *Quality into the 21st century—Perspectives on quality, competitiveness and sustained performance.* ASQ: A Quality Press.

Ramanathan, N. (2021). Quality-based management for future-ready corporations serving society and planet. *Total Quality Management & Business Excellence*, *3*(5–6), 541–557.

Ravitch, D. (2010). *The death and life of the great American school system: How testing and choice are undermining education.* Basic Books.

Rill, B. (2016). Resonant co-creation as an approach to strategic innovation. *Journal of Organizational Change Management*, *29*(7), 1135–1152.

Shaked, H., & Schechter, C. (2017). *Systems thinking for school leaders*: Holistic leadership for excellence in education. Springer.

Shingo Institute. (2017). *Shingo model*. Utah State University.

Snyder, K., Ingelsson, P., & Bäckström, I. (2018). Using design thinking to support value-based leadership for sustainable quality development. *Business Process Management Journal, 24*(6), 1289–1301.

Snyder, K. J. (2019). Preparing globally competent students: The K–12 schooling challenge. *Advances in Global Education and Research—GLOCER*, (3), 126–135.

Snyder, K. J., Acker-Hocevar, M., & Snyder, K. M. (2000, 2008). *Living on the edge of chaos: Leading schools into the global age* (1st and 2nd ed.). ASQ: A Quality Press.

Snyder, K. J., & Snyder, K. M. (2021). Building sustainable systems for schooling in turbulent times: Big ideas from the sciences. In Jeffrey Glanz (Ed.), *Crisis and pandemic leadership: Implications for meeting the needs of students, teachers and parents*. Rowman & Littlefield.

Snyder, K. M. (2007). The European quality benchmark system: Helping teachers to work with information to sustain change. *European Journal of Education, 42*(3), 425–435.

Snyder, K. M., Johnson, M., & Snyder, K. J. (2021). Going hybrid on a dime: Lessons from schooling during the pandemic and implications for sustainable quality in education. Paper presented at the 14th Annual International Conference on Education, Research and Innovation, Sevilla, Spain, November 8–10, 2021.

Suarez, F. F., & Montes, J. S. (2020) Building organisational resilience to cope and thrive in uncertain times, develop scripted routines, simple rules and the ability to improvise. *Harvard Business Review*. November–December.

Tinsley, C. H., & Ely, R. J. (2021, May–June). What most people get wrong about men and women. *Harvard Business Review*.

Uhl-Bien, M., & Arena, M. (2018). Leadership for organizational adaptability: A theoretical synthesis and integrative framework. *The Leadership Quarterly, 29*(1), 89–104.

UNESCO. (2017). *Education for sustainable development goals*. UNESCO.

Van Kemenade, E., & Hardjono, T. W. (2019). Twenty-first century total quality management: The emergence paradigm. *The TQM Journal, 31*(2).

Westling Allodi, M. (2013). Simple-minded accountability measures create failing schools in disadvantage contexts: A case study of a Swedish junior high school. *Policy Futures in Education, 11*(4), 331–363.

Chapter Three

A Quantum Worldview of Responsive Power for Sustainable Learning

Michele Acker-Hocevar

We often fail to see how our present power relationships hold us captive from making deep structural changes needed for sustainable learning that can yield very different educational outcomes. By choosing to socially construct power around a quantum worldview of systems thinking, coupled with network power and ethical principles of behavior, we can alter educational outcomes and frame responsive power within the potential of unleashing quantum power.

Quantum power is the result of quantum entanglement that describes a state where social actors interact and share a common set of beliefs, values, and attitudes that guide their actions to make decisions independent of others while simultaneously influencing others by their actions. Einstein termed these interactions as spooky actions at a distance because time and space did not diminish the entanglement of these ideas among members (Duarte, 2019).

The purpose of this chapter is to unravel how quantum power might develop. Leaders play a central and educative role to unleash it within the system's natural energy for it to flourish. Part 1 will illustrate how leaders can frame power relationships within a quantum worldview of systems thinking and network power (Capra & Luisi, 2014; Castells, 2000) and promote increased awareness of choices to level hierarchies that lead to quantum power.

Part 2 will describe what responsive power can do to build positive energy for both individual and organizational agency for increased engagement, a prerequisite of quantum power. Part 3 will compare and contrast power relationships in hierarchies and networks.

PART 1: RESPONSIVE POWER WITHIN A QUANTUM WORLDVIEW

Systems thinking lies at the heart of responsive power, which leads to quantum power. "Systems thinking is defined in terms of relationships, patterns, and context" (Capra & Luisi, 2014, p. xii). As such, viewing power as a system of roles and relationships from both hierarchical and network patterns, relationships, and contexts examines two very different worldviews of power for adaptation, innovation, and change (Ferguson, 2018).

Manuel Castells (2000) describes in his book *The Rise of the Network Society*, "a number of major social, technological, economic and cultural transformations [which] came together to give rise to a new form of society" (p. 17). This society is powered by microelectronic-based information that is decentralized and instantaneous. It is within this new organizational form that information processing, innovation, and knowledge creation are the keys to responsive power (Andersen, 2020). But that is not the entire picture. Responsive power is opportunity power for creating sustainable learning communities. It is a choice.

Different worldviews of power might shape dramatically dissimilar responses within an individual, classroom, team, school, district, and community. These different worldviews can shift power to a greater quantum worldview of responsive power or double down on hierarchy and bureaucratic control. Responsive power can become quantum power when it is unleashed within the organization with the possibility to raise the consciousness of all members to embrace their interconnected relationships around a higher purpose of ethical action (Laloux, 2014).

Embracing power mindsets challenges existing worldviews, for it removes labels that separate us, labels that are deeply derogatory and punitive in intent, and labels that are exclusionary in thinking rather than inclusionary (Acker-Hocevar & Touchton, 2001). Laible (2000) suggests a worldview of love, compassion, and acceptance—or a loving epistemology that is diametrically opposed to organizational patterns of isolation, judgment, and control. This worldview moves beyond responsive power to a quantum power deeply rooted in spirituality (Schwartz, 2017).

Importantly, responsive power is a choice each of us can make in terms of how we want to cement together our understanding of how to create sustainable learning in relationships. We can choose to be part of the whole fabric of the organization for positive and more democratic change, or we can psychologically withdraw from the organization and disengage ourselves, rendering the perpetuation of power over ideas to be left in the hands of a few who will shape the narratives for many (Andersen, 2020; Snyder et al., 2000, 2008).

Power is the big question about how our present educational systems can incorporate a quantum worldview of responsive power that levels hierarchies within systems thinking and organizational networks to promote sustainable learning. Leaders, however, will have to dance in both worlds of hierarchy and networks. In other words, this is not an either/or proposition but more of a conscious mind shift toward systems thinking and network organizational structures while recognizing that bureaucracies are not going away any time soon, nor will hierarchies of some type cease to exist (Ferguson, 2018).

This would be naïve. If hierarchy and bureaucracy are the main contexts of the leader's work, however, compliance will be the expected outcome and creative responses to adaptive change minimal (Acker-Hocevar, Ballenger, et al., 2012). Over time, other problems will arise as a cumulative non-responsiveness to changing conditions will yield an increased disconnect. It is highly likely that a sense of organizational inertia or personal and organizational powerlessness can lead to despair and hopelessness and even system collapse as members withdraw to survive.

Within processes of responsive power are behaviors that support collaborative and democratic partnerships of achieving sustainable learning by leveling hierarchies (Schoorman & Acker-Hocevar, 2010; Snyder et al., 2000, 2008). Because educators intuitively understand to level the playing field, they must seek to minimize hierarchies and create greater access for disadvantaged and disenfranchised groups to have needed resources. They do this by enhancing opportunities for everyone to live and to develop within sustainable learning communities better integrated within the whole of society (Acker-Hocevar, Cruz-Janzen, et al., 2012).

Although networks can foster connections with ideas that are beneficial and positive, they can also foster ideas that are divisive and negative (Castells, 2009). That is why it is necessary to view power responsiveness within a quantum worldview (Snyder et al., 2000). There really is no middle path forward. Educators must confront beliefs about power, for failure to do so will influence the future.

The big question for leaders today then is how to frame power relationships within what we know about contemporary organizations. Understanding how to frame sustainable learning within systems thinking and network power changes how leaders enact power relationships. It alters relationships. It builds on what we know about work today. In the organizational literature, this is simply called "fit."

In a quantum worldview, roles and relationships are the drivers that can forge connections for building a culture of continuous learning, stimulating self-organization through network thinking, and advancing new ideas to promote fresh strategies and innovation. Democratic practices can emerge through partnerships across role groups. Responsive power can enable individuals, teams, and the organization to coevolve by embracing "becoming" as a continual process of life. Power can move freely "through" the system by connecting with others around ideas and shared values that undergird actions to promote growth.

In a quantum worldview, power is not vested solely in a person, albeit each person possesses power, but rather, it is vested in a set of ideas that govern ethical behaviors of connectedness, partnerships, and democratic practices in a networked system. Importantly, ideas can also form a counternarrative, or a resistance mindset, to perceived hegemonic forces of power over ideas that generate fear, propagate a story of winners and losers, and spread misinformation (Capra & Luisi, 2014).

Members can commit to the ideals of sustainable learning for all and agree to adhere to the rules that govern behaviors (Castells, 2011) through ethical principles of trust, integrity, honesty, and respect for diversity from different points of view. Context matters and one size does not fit all (Acker-Hocevar & Touchton, 2006). Purposive action can promote shared beliefs, attitudes, values, and behaviors that support sustainable learning—learning that is generative, integrated, ongoing, and applicable to everyday life around real problems.

In a quantum worldview, responsive power does not mean doing more with less, but it does mean doing better with what we have. It is the quality of the relationships where everyone realizes that simply having more of what doesn't work will fail to yield different results. Slowing down and reflecting on action is an action; seeing reactionary actions as counterproductive signals something is askew. Learning is ongoing and learning how to learn is important.

In a quantum worldview, life's uncertainty and challenges are met through the strength of our connections with others of like minds around shared values, beliefs, attitudes, and behaviors that guide ethical decision-making and purposive actions (Touchton et al., 2012). Our entanglement forms a group consciousness that promotes unity around the diversity of ideas.

PART 2: WHAT RESPONSIVE POWER DOES

Moving to a quantum worldview of responsive power makes some assumptions about what leaders need to do to understand how they learned about power. Recognizing personal and organizational power narratives is essential at all levels to create and encourage responsive power around a shared understanding of what power means in systems thinking and network power.

Therefore, as leaders design sustainable learning communities, they are called upon to model responsive power and assess how their actions may contradict, confuse, and often retard responsive power, resulting in conflicting signals about how power is enacted and negotiated. An agreed-upon set of principles guides all members to reflect on their actions within a quantum worldview of responsive power. Everyone is accountable to the principles.

Although educators, as a group, don't necessarily think about responsive power in relationships as worldviews, these relationships, however, underpin certain recognizable patterns. For example, when power is being used over them to shape narratives and reward behaviors, members may feel resentment and exert passive resistance. Members may also understand that rhetoric does not reflect the reality of what the leaders say with what they do. Confronting behaviors that lack congruence and go against an agreed-upon set of principles that govern various relationships should not be seen as insubordinate but as helpful feedback.

Responsive power in a quantum worldview focuses on the unity of purpose for sustainable learning around a set of agreed-upon principles. Sustainable learning can be understood in terms of what this means for the organization to grow and develop to achieve its purpose. It should also be seen as individuals learning new behaviors. Obviously, a new teacher or a beginning principal should not be expected to be at the same level of development as a seasoned veteran. It is also essential to provide multiple forms of support for educators at all levels and to acknowledge that changing assumptions about relationships takes time.

Although certain types of interactions promote a unity of purpose by sharing ideas with the potential to generate and sustain learning within and across individuals, each person will be on their own journey. Foundational to this journey are beliefs that incorporate partnership thinking and democratic practices (Snyder et al., 2000). Unity rests on hearing and listening to others while operating within agreed-upon boundaries established within each network (Acker-Hocevar & Schoorman, 2006). This does not mean promoting sameness, but rather, it opens the door for the diversity of thought to flourish and for different ways to contribute.

Significantly, network communication has the potential to stimulate creativity for the extraordinary to emerge by unlocking the door to possibilities (Castells, 2009). A possibility is the natural synthesis of ideas that can result when individuals engage freely in dialogue and collaboration. When members are free to examine meaningful approaches to address systemic problems—exploring multiple ways to optimize resources and connections within and across various contexts—progress is possible.

Additionally, context influences the way leaders develop their personal and organizational power (Acker-Hocevar & Touchton, 2006). Some organizations may exhibit high levels of responsive power whereas other organizations may need more nurturing. If the organization has been top down, the change in power relationships will signal a different way forward. Patience will be necessary. Learning is a process. If educators thought that the only way to access power and gain influence is to rise in the hierarchy, what does this portend for others?

Rather, power reconstituted within a flattened hierarchy calls for high levels of personal power to be actualized. Hence, leaders help each person understand that they possess the personal power and potential to generate their own discursive narratives to alter reality—to create more space for themselves and others to practice responsive power—power that is an opportunity to be heard; power that is an opportunity to be creative and adaptive; power that is an opportunity to examine deeply rooted beliefs, attitudes, values, and behaviors that are generative and advance sustainable learning, systems thinking, and network connections.

The journey in learning about personal power is not just one story, static in time, but an evolving story. The story will change as new patterns of interaction emerge to transform relationships among members. Although in hierarchical and bureaucratic systems, "followers" may wait for signals from above to make decisions, trusting bonds in a network organization encourage individuals to respond in situ. This allows for more autonomy in decision making.

Because there is an assumption that decision making is coupled with responsible accountability and ethical principles that guide actions, individuals are free to respond to issues in real time. In other words, each network reflects the values and ethical principles that guide decision making. Each person understands their use of personal power in this trusting relationship to identify problems and look for systemic causes by studying the system. Everyone is a knowledge producer.

Engagement and ethical principles are critical in guiding these interactions within the network. Staying focused on the purpose of the network for sustainable learning keeps everyone moving in the right direction. On one level, leaders might promote bonds with others that strengthen open and honest communication, abandon labels and judgment, and encourage diverse points of view. On another level, leaders can disallow any person to force their ideas on another through intimidation or bullying. Leaders can expect that everyone has a stake in problem solving.

Although each network develops its own identity around its purpose and agreed-upon foundational principles for participation within and across the networks, the rules that govern interactions are culturally driven. Leaders may spearhead what these principles are for clarifying interactions among members within and across network hubs and how they can translate rules to enable congruent actions. But leaders will engage others in this process of collaboratively coming up with the rules. They will encourage the regular use of visuals, printed materials, and agreed-upon guidelines, particularly ethical principles, as touchstones.

Each member of the network accepts personal responsibility and accountability for their adherence to shared and agreed-upon values and principles of operation within the network. All members understand how they use responsive power in the decision-making process for sustainable learning where everyone has something to contribute to the system. Asking for help is not a weakness but a strength. Hence, responsive power creates communicative pathways for a person to want to share ideas, ask for what they need, offer assistance where they can provide service, and initiate novel approaches to solve seemingly intractable problems.

Rather than ignoring power, educators must embrace it and reflect daily on how the quality of their power interactions with others is either a facilitating force "through" the system (responsive power actions) or a constricting force "over" the system (hierarchy, i.e., control over actions). Power should energize. If it drains people of their natural energy for adaptive responses, then something is awry. Professionals should have the freedom to make decisions within their purview and around the unity of shared purpose and guidelines that govern behaviors.

Leaders must illustrate what this means and show where the organization is in relation to moving forward with accountability built into the system. When educators pay attention to the qualitative personal measures of growth in the system such as interpersonal and intrapersonal aspects of power, they can assess how these aspects impact overall organizational power. Some interpersonal aspects of personal power may include respect, listening, openness, cooperation, trust, reliability, honesty, learning, and innovation. Some intrapersonal aspects may include reflection, responsibility, resilience, exploration, dependability, and resourcefulness.

As organizational power grows, others see the strength of network connections that integrate services around system goals and provide a basis for the ongoing evaluation of holistic system performance (Snyder et al., 2000, 2008). An appraisal of how systemic research in lieu of knowledge creation and knowledge utilization changes how practice might also be examined.

Consequently, just as the above-listed positive indicators of personal and organizational power can be assessed in terms of the quality of the relationships and the impact on systemic learning overall, there are negative indices of personal and organizational power that can also be assessed. Ideally, the quality and health of relationships that promote personal responsibility in areas such as ongoing learning and participation should be reviewed in an ongoing basis.

To reiterate, as social actors, we learn from and with each other. We also learn from reflection and circling back to think individually and collectively about what could have been improved. Gossip and rumors may attempt to make sense of the workplace, while justification of poor performance by using a blame mindset may show a lack of personal responsibility and institutional isolation may insulate members from what is relevant, but any one of these, and all of them, are not productive and problematic.

Generating new ideas for collective action and agency for better decisions around a shared purpose and goals of sustainable learning within a quantum worldview of responsive power is not a static process. Involvement is critical. Scanning the environment for broader patterns within social, economic, and political trends is part of having responsive power. Responsive power focuses on opportunities to grow and develop self and others through access to information and resources. With a mature mindset, individuals are open to new possibilities.

PART 3: POWER RELATIONSHIPS IN HIERARCHIES AND NETWORKS

Simply put, power is its own energy force within a system—*any system*. Capra and Luisi (2014) state, "Power, in the sense of domination over others, is excessive self-assertion. The social structure in which it is exerted most effectively is the hierarchy" (p. 13). They further elaborate that individuals define themselves in relation to their position in the hierarchy and a "shift to a different system of values generates existential fears in them" (p. 13). But they also identify with another kind of power.

This other kind of power that Capra and Luisi (2014) suggest aligns with an ecological (holistic) paradigm is networks. They hint that "network hubs with the richest connections become centers of power" (p. 14) because of what is known as extending reach to the most people possible around ideas that bind them together (i.e., entanglement). Subsequently, the use of network power can be used over others in the network and over others in different networks (Castells, 2011), or preferably through people in the network and with others in different networks.

The bottom line is that the network that exerts the most *reach*, not through positional power (hierarchy) but through its ability to connect "more of the network to itself" (Capra & Luisi, 2014, p. 14), because of ideas builds iterative feedback loops into its structure for purposive actions for sustainable learning. When these connections build iterative feedback loops that reinforce deeply held values, quantum power emerges.

This does not occur in a hierarchy of top-down, one-way communication that ignores how important it is to have open, fluid, multidirectional communicative processes in place for ideas to flourish throughout the system. In responsive power, reach is about keeping everyone involved, informed, and extending the invitation to participate. It is about how meaningful work encourages engagement and strong connections for responsive action that unleashes quantum power to achieve desired educational outcomes.

Without more democratic processes to foster wider engagement within an understanding of a partnership power around shared values (Snyder et al., 2000, 2008), a vacuum can easily be filled with erroneous information as gossip and rumors attempt to make sense of uncertainty. Subsequently, leaders play an enormous role in sense-making (Weick, 1995) to fill the vacuum where misinformation might occur and refocus members on the opportunities for sustainable learning around purposive action.

Leaders can also create the means for redirecting and reminding members to practice ethical principles of behavior. They do this by having a framework of norms, values, and beliefs, with examples of successful behaviors that reinforce what is important. They also do this by being exemplary role models. In the words of Capra and Luisi (2014), a leader can create disequilibrium by altering power relationships in living systems. They state,

> Living systems, then, respond to disturbances from the environment autonomously with structural changes—that is, by rearranging their patterns of connectivity. According to Maturana and Varela, we can never direct a living system; we can only disturb it. More than that, the living system not only specifies its structural changes; it also specifies which disturbances from the environment trigger them. In other words, a living system has the autonomy to discriminate between what to notice and what will disturb it. (p. 256)

This is where the leader plays a vital role as mentioned above in sense-making and reminding members of the shared norms, values, beliefs, and ethical principles that support responsive power and can result in quantum power. Additionally, and following this line of thinking about sense-making, structural changes in a system are "acts of cognition" that bring forth a world, or in this chapter, a worldview that results in quantum power through understanding the energy of positive entanglement through a rich sharing of ideas in the network.

It makes sense, therefore, to see how "learning and development are merely two sides of the same coin" (Capra & Luisi, 2014, p. 256). When leaders encourage investigation of the whole and with others, everyone can see what patterns, relationships, and levels of connectedness exist, and how unique their context is for decisions about development. This truly is opportunity power. This process does not occur holistically within the hierarchy because a leader is expected to have all the answers, to supervise, and to evaluate while working in isolation.

With network power, the findings from an ongoing examination of the system can provide necessary information to disturb the system for everyone to learn and decide what needs attention. Power relationships within the hierarchy situate power outside the person. Simply put, power is something to be acquired through various means—it is not something that the person exercises freely.

In a hierarchy, political actors employ various partisan strategies to build pacts that increase access to control resources over opportunities through policies, procedures, and legislation that limit democratic practices (Andersen, 2020). Misinformation and victimization silence those at the bottom of the hierarchy through fear, punishment, and isolation from the whole. This is not responsive power.

Hierarchical power limits engagement, stifles sustainable learning, and is often understood through such euphemisms as the person who has the gold makes the rules. It exemplifies why giving power up to those who hold it is so challenging (Andersen, 2020). This is a zero-sum game of power about control. Once responsive power lays the foundation for what becomes quantum power, hierarchy cannot control outcomes, and change becomes inevitable.

In network relationships, the power is in the network connections around shared values and beliefs that guide decision making and learning. There is an opportunity to explore what might be possible, to have a voice, and to be a leader. Networks may have the face of one leader, but everyone has the power to contribute freely to ideas that shape the actions of the network as a whole. Everyone matters.

There are numerous ways to be heard without criticism and fear of reprisal. People are not attacked but ideas can be questioned. Nothing is personal. It is about understanding how to share ideas respectfully. Schools organized around network structures provide opportunity power for everyone to learn in a more open and democratic way.

Although we know that hierarchy exists in the natural world in terms of promoting cooperation—and it is not the raw notion of "survival of the fittest," as most of us thought—we may not understand what this means in a quantum worldview (Capra & Luisi, 2014). Survival within a natural system is about the cooperation of living things working together to find how best to grow, develop, and adapt to engender survival. It is completely contrary to a hierarchical view of control over access to opportunities and resources as competitive. Networks, by definition, tend to be cooperative. Access to information is open.

Without cooperation, social or human systems can become maladaptive over time. For reasons that are many and include such things as greed, selfishness, disinformation, control, and a simple disregard for how decisions today may affect short-term and long-term outcomes tomorrow, more and more people are questioning how this type of social control over information and resources serves sustainability (Andersen, 2020). Many suggest it does not.

Hierarchy is the antithesis of quantum power and learning; it negates systems thinking of connections and wholeness; it pits one group against another; it makes those on the bottom know they are the bottom. It lacks a higher moral purpose of raising up everyone to reach their greatest potential. It makes sense today to view network power as a more organic form of responding cooperatively and promoting this organizational structure to nurture sustainable learning and responsive power within a systems view.

Intentional actions of a community linked together tightly through entanglement can determine collectively what to pay attention to, and what patterns in the past we have paid homage to that no longer serve us well. These may be patterns we choose to rid ourselves from as we adopt new structures within a quantum worldview of a responsive power mindset.

In other words, if we believe in a sense of responsive power, then these patterns of power relationships should look more like an upside-down pyramid. Co-participation of multiple actors forms the base of the pyramid. And through entanglement, educators can find solutions to problems to create futures of hope that transform each of us because of shared values and beliefs.

Historically, and even more recently as stated previously, we can see how patterns of power in hierarchies are suspect in our institutions. The one-size-fits-all approach of hegemonic solutions, which ignores contextual variety and diversity patterns, is under scrutiny. Quick fixes in the form of mandates, often punitive to the most vulnerable groups, are under review. This failure to question real systemic causes underlying a worldview of ranking systems from best to worst is lamentable. It only serves to further disenfranchise and label those who are already the most vulnerable among us (Acker-Hocevar & Touchton, 2001).

It appears, therefore, that a basis for sustainable schooling to thrive means questioning the very idea of leadership in a hierarchy where one person is in charge and where labels divide us. In a network, there is an awareness and acceptance of everyone as a leader—but at different times. Everyone has the power to take on leadership roles. Successful leaders have always understood leadership as relational and task oriented. The difference today is that leaders bring forth a dense leadership network of members who practice responsive power collectively within the bounds of the network and systems thinking.

Moving to quantum power requires that leaders connect decision making and action to a higher ethical purpose. Ongoing professional development, rich networks of multiple leaders, and rapid advances in technology can incorporate timely responses and ongoing feedback around results for purposive behaviors to flourish. When information comes from people who are trusted and this information aligns with the values and core identity and purpose of the system, actions can be swift.

This means network communication is a skill that can be learned and fostered to promote and influence—yes, to persuade, others about ideas. Responsive power within an organization is the result of how trustworthy leaders are viewed and how they communicate and translate cherished values dear to the community for collective action to ensue.

Just as transformational leadership is around a higher moral purpose, the power that is transformational means leaders help others know what to pay attention to. They bring people together around what connects them to move beyond compliance. Thus, when educators communicate this higher purpose, it engenders closer ties with community members and establishes a willingness to partner with educators to address problems (Acker-Hocevar, Cruz-Janzen, et al., 2012). And when this communication fosters connections around a shared, higher purpose, educators and their communities are models of possibility and hope.

CONCLUSION: A CALL FOR ACTION

Power is the big question in our relationships today (Andersen, 2020) as we move from hierarchy to network organizations. Leaders must differentiate power relationships within systems thinking and network organizations compared with fragmented bureaucratic and hierarchical organizations. Self and organizational readiness and awareness of knowledge and skills needed for a quantum worldview of responsive power is the first step toward sustainable learning.

After this initial assessment, leaders have members develop a path forward. A conceptual framework is shared about how the different pieces of responsive power fit together to engender quantum power. Leaders free members to focus on a continuous process of development, learning, and becoming. Using benchmarks, individual, network, and organizational assessments, leaders create a culture of ongoing feedback about where members are in the process. Leaders must let go of how the journey unfolds and remind others of the higher purpose of what they do together to promote unity and engagement.

REFERENCES

Acker-Hocevar, M., Ballenger, J., Place, W., & Ivory, G. (Eds.). (2012). *Snapshots of school leadership in the 21st century: Perils and promises of leading for social justice, school improvement, and democratic community (The UCEA Voices from the Field Project).* UCEA sponsored publication. Information Age Publishers

Acker-Hocevar, M., Cruz-Janzen, M., Schoon, P., Supran, E., Walker, D., & Wilson, C. (2003, April). *Questions of sustainable school progress and the politics surrounding poverty and limited English proficiency.* Paper accepted for presentation at the meeting of the American Educational Research Association, Chicago, IL.

Acker-Hocevar, M., Cruz-Janzen, M. I., & Wilson, C. L. (2012). *Leadership from the ground up: Sustainable school improvement in traditionally low performing schools.* Information Age Publishers.

Acker-Hocevar, M., Cruz-Janzen, M. I., Wilson, C. L., Schoon, P., & Walker, D. (2005). The need to re-establish schools as dynamic positive human energy systems that are non-linear and self-organizing: The learning partnership tree. *International Journal of Learning, 12.*

Acker-Hocevar, M., & Schoorman, D. (2006, April). *Building democratic faculty governance as critical decision making: The politics of listening and giving voice.* Paper proposal for presentation at the annual meeting of the American Educational Association (AERA), San Francisco, CA.

Acker-Hocevar, M., & Touchton, D. (2001, April). *Principals' struggle to level the accountability playing field of Florida graded "D" and "F" schools in high poverty and minority communities.* (Report No. UD 034 535). Teachers College, Columbia University: Institute for Urban and Minority Education (ERIC No. ED 458 322).

Acker-Hocevar, M., & Touchton, D. (2006, April). *Contextual leadership: Using case studies to demonstrate how schools are responding to social justice issues in high-risk schools.* Paper proposal for presentation at the annual meeting of the American Educational Association (AERA), San Francisco, CA.

Acker-Hocevar, M., & Touchton, D. (2011). A model of power as social relationships: Teacher leaders describe the phenomena of effective agency in practice. In Eleanor Blair Hilty (Ed.), *Teacher leadership: The "new" foundations of education* (pp. 239–264). Peter Lang Publishers.

Andersen, K. (2020). *Evil geniuses the unmaking of America: A recent history.* Penguin Press.

Capra, F., & Luisi, P. L. (2014). *The systems view of life: A unifying vision.* Cambridge University Press.

Castells, M. (2000). *The rise of the network society.* Blackwell Publishers.

Castells, M. (2009). *Communication power.* Oxford University Press.

Castells, M. (2011). A network theory of power. *International Journal of Communication, 5*, 773–778.

Duarte, F. J. (2019). *Fundamentals of quantum entanglement.* Institute of Physics.

Ferguson, N. (2018). *The square and the tower: Networks and power, from the Freemasons to Facebook.* Penguin Press.

Laible, J. C. (2000). A loving epistemology: What I hold critical in my life, faith and profession, *International Journal of Qualitative Studies in Education, 13*(6), 683–692.

Laloux, F. (2014). *Reinventing organizations: A guide to creating organizations inspired by the next stage in human consciousness.* Parker Nelson.

Schwartz, M. (2017). *The possibility principle.* Sounds True.

Schoorman, D., & Acker-Hocevar, M. (2010). Viewing faculty governance within a social justice framework: Struggles and possibilities for democratic decision-making in higher education. *Equity & Excellence in Education, 43*(3), 310–325.

Snyder, K. J., Acker-Hocevar, M., & Snyder, K. M. (2000, 2008). *Living on the edge of chaos: Leading schools into the global age.* ASQ The Quality Press.

Touchton, D., & Acker-Hocevar, M. (2011, Summer). Decision-making quandaries that superintendents face in their work in small school districts building democratic communities. *Journal of Public Relations, 32*(3), 210–236.

Touchton, D., Taylor, R., & Acker-Hocevar, M. (2012). Decision-making processes, giving voice, listening, and involvement. In M. Acker-Hocevar, J. Ballenger, W. Place, & G. Ivory (Eds.), *Snapshots of school leadership in the 21st century: Perils and promises of leading for social justice, school improvement, and democratic community (The UCEA Voices From the Field Project)* (pp. 121–145). UCEA sponsored publication. Information Age Publishers.

Weick, K. (1995). *Sensemaking in organizations.* Sage Publishers.

Chapter Four

The Quantum School Leader as a Strategic Systems Thinker

Elaine C. Sullivan

This chapter shares a story of developing the *Quantum Strategic School Leadership* (QSSL) model for thinking about how to influence school change and development for sustainability purposes. The model is based on knowledge from the sciences of systems thinking, positive psychology, and quantum, chaos, and complexity theories. The model grew out of my continued research and reflections about school leadership over the past 45 years.

The intent is to provide the QSSL knowledge and framework to expand one's view and expertise on how to think and influence strategically and holistically for school leadership to prepare students to thrive in a changing global society. The story of learning to become a leader is told as an example of integrating cognitive, emotional, spiritual, and physical intelligence in developing leadership qualities.

Today's leaders face very different conditions than in the past, made more pressing by the increasing acceleration rate and volume of change, causing volatility, uncertainty, complexity, and ambiguity (VUCA), a U.S. Army War College acronym. Global trends such as technological advancements, migrations, and pandemics disrupt the economy, environment, and society. COVID-19 shows that rapid and intense change can occur swiftly, causing upheaval in our lives, and often creating feelings of disorder, fear, and control. Today's organizations need a kind of leadership that complements working in VUCA circumstances (Elkington et al., 2017).

Schools are no longer isolated from outside trends. In an emergent context, QSSL blends a "bubble up" and "trickle down" approach to leadership that accesses all energy, passion, and commitment. This energy fuels the fires of systems thinkers to take strategic action for flourishing in an unpredictable world. Adapting for sustainability in emergent times requires thinking holistically and strategically, making QSSL well-matched for leading.

THE QUANTUM WORLDVIEW

The quantum universe allows individuals to choose their identity and influence their path to be one that is full of promise, learning, hopefulness, and affirmation, or one of despair and no control (Wheatley, 2017). The quantum worldview values self-awareness, purpose, meaning, trust, ethics, connectedness, integration, potential, and servant behavior. Holistic is where the parts work together instead of a fragmented one with parts functioning separately.

The quantum approach includes everyone accessing the potential pool of energy, ideas, information, and buy-in to create meaning for adapting for sustainability. Quantum principles create a worldview of looking at the whole from an integrated perspective to think about how to use its networks, energy, and relationships to foster sustainability (Tsao & Laszlo, 2019; Wheatley, 2017; Zohar, 1997, 2016).

Quantum thinking integrates intelligence, such as mental, emotional, spiritual, and physical, to create a holistic, diverse, and "both-and" perspective. Intentionally developing self-awareness and mindfulness builds intuition, foresight, and strategic intent as part of the thinking processes. These senses tap into the system's energy of the in-between spaces, the white space, to influence working toward the shared purpose (Tsao & Laszlo, 2019; Zohar, 2016).

QSSL is a perspective on how to "think about thinking" on how to influence people to think strategically and systemically to take actions for sustainable positive schooling, which is quantum thinking. It facilitates strategic short- and long-term change in an integrated leadership system that emphasizes the dynamics of relationships and processes to build energy, knowledge, and capacities to create innovation and sustainability.

The premise is that leadership is a complex adaptive system (CAS) where the whole is greater than its interdependent and interconnected parts. Leadership consists of a formal leader(s) and followers working together to lead by intentional thinking, learning, influencing, and inspiring for making continuous adaptation in the larger school context. Including everyone in all the processes generates many creative possibilities for the highest leverage points of change. All viewpoints are accepted, creating a pluralistic mindset that taps into the potential for the system to respond to its environment.

PART 1: THE EMERGENCE OF THE QUANTUM STRATEGIC SCHOOL LEADERSHIP MODEL

This section lifts up insights from experiences that connect quantum and complexity principles to the change process that emerged during a self-awareness journey. These insights linked with research resulted in my development of the quantum strategic school leadership model with examples from my path offered for others to relate to and learn about the quantum strategic leadership dimensions. My story is shared as an illustration to inspire others to choose to make the journey of learning to know oneself better to discover their leadership talents.

The path for each is different with diverse experiences and impacts, yet the journey has the same basic processes. The mindful way of coming to know oneself is through learning about and reflecting on experiences and knowledge for defining new behaviors for practice, in this case, leadership gifts. Becoming more self-aware is about attuning to personal beliefs, a congruence between one's inner and outer self in the act of becoming whole or being in sync, the guiding core to action. Reflection and mindfulness about experiences are pivotal for deciding one's leadership, followership, and life role for a harmonious, healthy, and productive life.

A Journey to Strategic Living

Farming and ranching are not jobs; instead, it is a way of life, thinking, and being. It is my way of living, thinking, and being! A specific life view comes from being raised on a ranch and farm, where the norm is practicality, creativity, connections, innovation, perseverance, independent thinking, continuous self-directed learning, and community. Knowledge from agricultural research, experts, experiences, and many sources establish a multi-view for thinking about deliberate actions and how to adapt to grow crops or raise cattle in the short and long term.

I intentionally thought about how my farm and ranch life experiences and practices might relate to my career roles to become an effective teacher, counselor, principal, and person. In farming and ranching, everything is viewed as a connected living system within a more extensive system where the environmental conditions and human actions make a difference in success or failure. Farming and ranching have to be "in sync" with nature as a whole system to be sustainable, that is, to continue to exist. Sustainability happens when the farmer constantly thinks about the "Big Picture," with the segments working together for the growth of the whole.

Failure is probable if the farmer handles the parts of the whole as a stand-alone, either for the short or long term. Farming is also trial and error, an iterative process with sustainability occurring when the system adapts due to the parts working together. "Seeing the Big Picture" as a way of thinking about leadership and the school as a whole of interrelated and interdependent parts that adapt and learn made sense to me, just as it did for running the farm and ranch.

Farm sustainability occurs from adaptation, which requires strategic thinking and acting in the day-to-day and long-term farm operations. Change happens from the possible daily disruptions from broken equipment, bad weather, mistakes in following crop fertilizer directions, or cattle medications. In the long term, change may happen due to climate change causing drought, excessive rain during haying season, shortage of cash flow, and many other possibilities. In the short term, dealing with change by adapting determines success or failure in a crop or cattle production while still moving towards sustainability.

Information determines actions to reduce or stimulate growth for a successful production with the consistent goal to produce a good crop at just the right time for the market or user, whether hay, watermelons, or cows. Successful crops or sales allow the farm to live for another day, the short term. Sustainability is the farm existing for the long term. Using information from many sources for short- and long-term decision making as occurred on the farm became integrated into my behaviors for leading a school for student personal growth and learning.

One of our annual rituals of ranch work during the winter months is to burn the wiregrass in the sandhills to stimulate the growth of more grass for the cattle. In controlled burns, small patches of grass are selected for burning based on the environmental conditions of wind and the area's surroundings. The patches of fire spread and then connect, taking off with great energy to change the desired location resulting in a new landscape of rich, fresh grass for the cattle within a few weeks.

Not all pastureland is burned, only the section needing rescue of dead grass and areas targeted for the improved forage. The fire does not destroy the site in question; it just becomes different. Patching in systems thinking work is modifying a part of a whole, a patch, of an existing system to stimulate change, just as in the controlled burn example. Modifying part of a system to promote overall growth became part of my thinking about how to stimulate individual and organizational change in small ways to leverage more significant change.

Through the generations, my huge extended family continues to live and work as a connected unit in the role of family and friends. Everyone's knowledge, ideas, experience, and perspective are brought forth for making informed choices, in essence, collaborating for work and life. I saw the power of a family community, a network, in pooling resources, knowledge, and emotional support in getting the job done.

The adage that one can choose one's friends but not one's relatives sets forth the need to work as a community for the well-being of the whole extended family, not that it was always easy or orderly! I knew that building a community mindset and using networks had to be the foundation of my values for living. My family held that learning is essential because knowledge is the key to power over a situation or people.

I noticed firsthand the differences in my learning experiences between my Dad's black farm workers, poor white kids, and even cousins. I observed my parents helping people gain power over themselves by providing opportunities to gain knowledge through learning and experiences. They offered opportunities, such as transportation, business advice, sewing clothes, meeting with college officials, and even financially. My Dad became a 24-year school board member to fight for equity for all.

My parents used the principles of nurturing personal growth to teach their four daughters about life's natural progressions, nature, and personal responsibility. Our parents encouraged us to be independent thinkers by being informed and accountable in making choices by our own will, instead of through someone else's pressure or opinion. My sisters and I were encouraged to check out all the possible alternatives before deciding on a course of action.

This concept of scanning the situation or environment for evaluating the multiple possible ways to take action for the greatest influence on others is a significant part of the decision-making process in the systems approach to living. Intuitively, I used this scanning method in my work and personal life, which I labeled and referred to as an "alternatives approach for making decisions."

The research on the impact of systems thinking helped me to know how this process worked even more effectively within a system as a whole in getting people to take action in facilitating change. Whether on the farm and ranch, in the family circle, or in social interactions, my parents understood that achieving one's full potential comes from having opportunities to make information into meaningful knowledge.

My upbringing shaped the belief that learning provides the power to imagine possibilities for choosing who one wants to be and can generate chances to achieve that identity. A fundamental freedom of living systems is to choose an identity (Wheatley, 2017). My parents believed acquiring and reflecting on knowledge and experiences led to personal growth, giving one the grit to write one's story to achieve that imagined life. They taught us to believe that knowledge is power and that learning is living!

DISCOVERING A LEADERSHIP PATH

As a developing educator, it quickly became evident that my thinking about how students learn did not align with how the school was organized and managed. It was important for students to acquire higher-order skills and be active learners to have power over themselves to choose their identity. My family upbringing and farm way of life pushed me to find unique means around these hurdles to become a teacher and eventually a counselor, which I believe made a difference.

As I forged my passage for actively participating in the system, I also planted the seeds of knowledge and experiences for others to gain another view about teaching and organizing. This effort to influence others is the start of my deliberate use of the strange attractor principle to cause purposely change. Strange attractors, and patterns, are powerful for influencing changes in a system's behavior, which matched up with my thoughts on using learning as a stimulus for change (Elkington et al., 2017).

As a teacher and high school counselor, I observed that schools used an autocratic, top-down approach in their organization and did not adapt to changing world conditions. Teachers used the same hierarchical authoritarian method that they complained about the school's management, as was also evident from the district's top-level to bottom-level practices (teachers). Schools functioned as closed systems with a pattern of hierarchical, autocratic management with no connections to the real world, except maybe for sports and band.

When I became a principal, I determined that under my leadership, a school would have an open system with work patterns that were based on collaboration and self-organization for decision-making. As a beginning principal, I started by using a participatory leadership perspective, a distributed leadership idea, which evolved to include strategic action and systems thinking practices. Scant literature and research existed on participatory leadership to guide my thinking and learning, especially about how to include everyone in the change process.

My certainty that if a change affects certain people they should be part of the solution, ensuring that my leadership had to be shared and purposeful. To this end, groups were established in and across grade levels to support participatory practices. I set a plan to study and observe any sources to gain information to support my leadership practices to influence organizational change. My formal and informal studies reinforced that building community establishes buy-in and motivation for taking action for the success of the student, themselves, and the organization.

In collaborative groups, staff advocated for what they thought was the best course of action, resulting in the group synthesizing ideas to form strategic intent to achieve. My organizing values of building community and using networks informed my thinking for using everyone's ideas, experiences, and input for the same reasons as on the farm because it worked. In both schools of my principalship, collaboration, networking, and participatory leadership produced the energy to facilitate and manage change. Collaboration patterns helped to establish a different kind of school culture.

Collaboration helped staff and stakeholders to realize why a change was needed, which integrated combined expertise and action for the school's progress. By everyone sharing, everyone sees the "Big Picture," and recognizes multiple possibilities that exist for addressing related issues. The farm and career experiences of observing the impact of the parts on the whole and vice versa pointed out the need to be in sync with the larger context of the world, life, and work. A bottom-up method of including staff in all the work processes accomplished more change and stability than previously with top-down leaders.

Increasing the collaboration at the elementary school occurred quickly and efficiently as it was common in their grades. In contrast, the transition to collaboration across grades, teams, and school-wide took longer. In high school, I had to create a collaborative work mindset by creating interdepartmental teams for dealing with school-wide issues. At first, changes occurred at the lower part of Maslow's needs hierarchy, addressing such matters as the labeling on the staff bathroom doors, times on traffic signs at the school entrance, and staff meal choices.

Initially, the staff learned that they did not have the skills to work in groups, which led to training in learning how to be an influential, responsible team member. Continuous learning, practice, and reflection led to a collaborative work culture and to the emergence of self-organization. My study and observations of the inclusion of everyone in the managing and leading processes revealed that there is greater potential for energy, knowledge, and abilities to make more valuable and productive change. Including all stakeholders increased buy-in for thinking about what and how to change, as well as increasing follow-through.

During my principalship, the pattern of teachers working isolated behind closed doors disappeared; instead, schools became a whole system of teachers working together for students. My schools achieved recognition, receiving many awards for their innovations. And I received many leadership awards, including becoming the 1997 Florida Principal of the Year and the 1998 National Principal of the Year for the United States.

Becoming a Quantum Strategic School Leader

The power of learning allows us to become unique leaders or responsible participants in leadership. This story about the convergence of highlights presents the deliberate process of knowing oneself in becoming a leader in developing leadership unique to one's personal beliefs and style. In expanding my self-awareness to guide my leadership development, I chose values, insights, and knowledge from my upbringing, life experiences on a ranch, and "habits" from my formal and informal career studies and training. My intentional choices guided the pursuit of relevant knowledge and professional development to learn about and reflect on leadership.

My reflection on leadership behaviors and processes guided me on how to influence the school to be relevant in changing times. My story, one example of many possible stories, is offered to encourage others to create their unique narrative through the shared iterative process vital for learning leadership, developing needed capacities, and expanding leadership perspective. The path is made by continuous study, practice, and reflection to connect leadership practices to life experiences, personal development, and informal and formal education.

My leadership presence emerged from personal and career experiences, studies, leader and counselor preparation, and the wisdom found in Bennis's seminal work *On Becoming a Leader* (1989). The most crucial aspect for developing one's unique leadership role and outlook is first to know oneself. Becoming self-aware of experiences helps create a value system and core beliefs for "thinking about thinking" for leading and living. Leaders need to be grounded in their personal vision, core values, and beliefs to lead others authentically (Zohar, 1997).

My core values of being in a community and organizing systems holistically led me to purposefully think about how to include everyone as a leader in facilitating whole system change. Mindfulness clarified for me the importance of the leader in promoting and supporting the conditions that motivate and prepare everyone to actively work for the good of the organization and the student.

Knowing oneself through self-awareness integrates the mind, body, and soul for a holistic self-view of integrated thinking. The head is for thinking about *the what*, the soul describes the *feelings and emotions*, and the body element is for *action*. The self's thinking roles need to be "in sync" to guide others effectively. Holistic thinking for leadership is gaining momentum in mainstream research. Laszlo's (2012) evolutionary leadership concept in systems work links the head and the heart for an integrated view in connecting lifelong learning, thinking, and emotion.

Laszlo's term *systems* means to connect the head and heart, which resonates with my QSSL perspective of leading with the head, body, and soul as a strategic systems thinker. Inquiry into what it takes to get an individual to take action or create energy for an organization gave rise to my thinking about "reading between the lines" of relationships about feelings and action or inaction. This between area cannot be seen and is defined as the white space of leadership, the invisible leadership, or leadership from the inside out. Leadership can be described and felt, yet often cannot be seen, is observable, and then not so observable (Daft & Lengel, 1998).

Study, practice, and reflection on my behaviors showed how this invisible leadership dimension could be better understood and used in leading. Giving attention to reading between the lines of interactions helped me know how to use white space more effectively. Understanding "the white space" is essential to thinking and leading, as using it causes inclusion to occur, which increases diversity. Diversity of thought produces the energy system for action. As a practice, I intentionally paid attention to gut feelings and coincidences, which can be thought of as intuition and perception, to learn how to think about using and trusting this use in leading.

The little-used senses of insight, perception, intuition, and foresight are critical aspects of quantum thinking. These senses are integrated into my thinking processes to access the white space of leadership that is fundamental in producing the emotional energy binding people together for going with the flow, which is vital for adaptive change. Each of us should become adept at using the white space for leading and living for the good of ourselves, the school, the people, and the planet.

From a very young age, I often intentionally thought about and analyzed my behavior and experiences to figure out how to think and act differently to influence the outcome during the next occurrence. Discovering that my introspective behavior matched up with the reflection process gave me valuable information on how to mindfully practice my thinking about thinking. More thoughtfully connecting my experiences and learnings to my behavior helped me unravel how to better handle and influence my life experiences and choices, and hopefully will do so for the reader.

My reflections gave me power, optimism, and hopefulness for guiding me in how to best lead and live. A positive, affirming relationship encourages others to participate in the thinking and leadership processes. The optimism in becoming a quantum strategic leader is described in the profound quote attributed to C. S. Lewis, a British writer and lay theologian: "You can't go back and change the beginning, but you can start where you are and change the ending."

THE QUANTUM STRATEGIC LEADERSHIP MODEL FOR SCHOOLS

My commitment to professional practice and my heart as a practitioner gave me the insights to be an active learner to ramp up effective leadership practices throughout my career. The collection of my written thoughts and learnings about leadership over more than three decades led to my growth in using a strategic leadership perspective. Studying the new sciences provided more information for a different way of thinking about organizational change and leadership that shifted my view of leadership and school organizations.

In this updated viewpoint, both are complex adaptive systems that exist in a symbiotic relationship nested in a more extensive interconnected system, much like a fractal organization. The new sciences clarified my thinking for including quantum and complexity principles in my leadership view, which resulted in my creating the quantum strategic school leadership concept and framework.

QSSL is the process of leading individually and collectively as a systems thinker for the future and the present for the "Big Picture" with strategic thought, intent, and action. The QSSL base comes from knowledge from the new sciences of complexity, chaos, and quantum theories, systems thinking, positive psychology, and the living sciences. Research from these fields set forth new thought patterns for understanding why situations are the way they are, the natural processes of change, and using emergence to effectively take action, interconnectivity, holism, self-organization, and collaboration.

Living on the Edge of Chaos (Snyder et al., 2000) suggests that change is expected, random, and constant, which causes disequilibrium, pushing the system to the edge of chaos. Quantum strategic thinking and acting are used in emergent conditions to identify strong interdependencies and connections to select the best leverage to create a tipping point in the change cycle.

Effective leadership includes everyone working together to analyze situations and contexts from many views for building multidimensional knowledge to create many possibilities. To self-organize is to adapt. A commitment to a clear sense of purpose and the cocreation of a vision drive all actions and processes. Cocreating a vision helps make sense of conditions by giving one direction and feelings of control to select the best leverage interventions. A unified purpose creates strength.

Leadership is a complex adaptive system of interconnected and intertwined parts with fractals, and patterns, reflecting the whole. The system's whole is a formal leader(s) role and followers, which focuses on processes, not the person in the leader role. Leadership is organic, with roles and functions emerging, shifting, and exchanging in different situations and settings. The system's energy emerges from the interactions of all relationships across the system. Quantum leaders use spirituality, consciousness, and values to form a mindset in a critical mass of participants to take adaptive action (Zohar, 2016).

QSSL uses a systems approach that embraces paradoxes for understanding and leveraging the change process. Quantum science specifies that paradoxes are inherent and valuable to an individual's and organization's development, where contradictions reflect the multiple realities found in quantum theories (Obolensky, 2010). Some of the paradoxes integral to QSSL and are needed are (1) leadership and followership, (2) leadership as a process and leader role as a position, (3) the school as a closed system and open system, (4) sustainability and innovation, (5) individual and organization, and (6) the leadership and management functions.

QSSL accepts each side and the middle space between the sides of a paradox to establish a mindset of "both-and" instead of the Newtonian "either-or" dictate. An "either-or" view that accepts just one side uses only 50% of available energy, information, and creativity in facilitating change limiting choices. A shift to "and-both" uses all the space of a paradox, creating a system rich with potential energy, commitment, knowledge, and creativity for thinking and acting about considering all possibilities to make the change. QSSL tapping into the whole continuum creates the potential of endless energy for adaptation in VUCA conditions.

Quantum Strategic School Leadership Clusters

Integrating mind, spirit, and body, a holistic approach to leadership includes everyone's thinking to discover possibilities for adapting to today's complex issues. Quantum strategic school leadership consists of four interconnected and interdependent clusters as presented in Table 4.1: (1) Discover the Possibilities and Challenges, (2) Facilitate the Dance of Change, (3) Together We Are Stronger, and (4) Lead with Soul.

Discover the Possibilities and Challenges Overview

This cluster's behavior set emphasizes using the mind to think about information to make decisions and select the appropriate strategies. The cognitive skills and agility for strategic systems thinking rely on open-mindedness, personal creativity, independent thinking, and self-directed learning. Cognitive ability and agility are essential for determining what the information means, interpreting conditions, how data will affect people, and how people may react to change (Capra & Luisi, 2014). An individual's power to influence

Table 4.1. The Four Clusters of Quantum Strategic School Leadership

Discover the Possibilities and Challenges	Facilitate the Dance of Change	Together We Are Stronger	Lead with Soul
• Co-Create a Clear Sense of Purpose and Vision • See the Big Picture with Systemic and Strategic Intent • Acquire and Connect Knowledge Across Disciplines • Examine One's Connection Systems • Analyze Conditions for Internal and External Change • Discover the Intervention Leverage Points	• Organize Leadership as Holistic, Process-Oriented, and Future-Based • Develop Strategic Systems Thinking Leadership Capability for All • Build Networks of Formal and Informal Relationships • Create Structures for Sustainability and Innovation • Embrace and Dance with Complexity for Transformation • Conduct Strategic Conversations to Mobilize for Change	• Live with a Positive Orientation to Life • Share in Leadership to Empower Self and Others • Be a Lifelong Learner across Disciplines • Self-Organize to Create Growth and Sustainability • Use Networks to Create Interconnections and Interdependence • Participate in Communities of Learning for Innovation	• Know Thyself and Establish a Personal Vision • Lead with Intention and Commitment • Be Passionate, Energetic, and Spirited • Guide with Principles and Ethics as a Servant Leader • Build and Sustain Relationships to Create Energy for Change • Lead from the Future with Possibilities Thinking

an individual and a system comes from acquiring and connecting knowledge across disciplines in leadership change.

Leadership facilitates the cocreation of all participants' vision for the imagined shared future that guides the school's development journey. Adaptive strategies are supported for stakeholders to have points of influence for the whole system to coevolve. The leadership lens for leveraging and facilitating growth considers how living systems act as a whole within a more extensive system.

This holistic perspective gives meaning to how leadership and the organization function during change, providing clues on how the system responds within processes, relationships, and all aspects to determine how to think about transforming (Wheatley, 2017). "Seeing the Big Picture" helps quantum strategic leaders provide leverage among all the system's parts of people, processes, and structures to generate intentional responsiveness and adaptiveness toward strategic intent.

Facilitate the Dance of Change Overview

Leaders in the Dance of Change awaken all individuals to think strategically and systemically to consider all the possibilities for improving schools. Leaders are viewed as energetic *doers* leading from an internal drive that infuses their actions with spirit, energy, and creativity. As a visionary and implementer, the leader straddles both the present and future worlds to promote strategic systems thinking to create a positive present bridge to the future.

The quantum leader creates processes and structures for innovation and sustainability, such as collaboration, networking, empowerment, and professional development. Leaders understand the power of these processes and structures in constructing meaning and purpose for the followers to produce buy-in and energy. Empowering people builds a culture of commitment and ownership of desiring to create the best for themselves, their students, and the school for the greater good.

Leaders continuously build a community to create energy and creativity to translate plans into action to mobilize staff. The leader always thinks and acts strategically to nurture formal and informal networks for collaboration to monitor and shape systems. Strategic conversations are used to encourage commitment and build a strategic plan. Storytelling forms a shared history to build a culture of translating ideas into action. The purposeful language of quantum leaders builds community, develops a common language, and a shared history that creates the energy and knowledge for thinking positively to support change for the future.

Together We Are Stronger Overview

QSSL strives to engage everyone, leader(s) and followers, and all stakeholders, in transforming schools into the most effective system for preparing students in the present while preparing them for an unknown future. Schools are people oriented; work occurs in socially organized structures to transmit knowledge to develop students. Leaders use the school's positive core, all its people, to influence and inspire them to willingly take action for the growth of the individual and the organization.

Everybody connecting establishes the shared meaning that forms the school's values, vision, and purpose to guide individual and collective actions for working in a natural change process. More people in leadership increases communication, making more opportunities for disturbances to the system, more opportunities for choosing to notice or not, and more opportunities to change conditions. Increased connections create the foundation for strategic thinking and action.

The view of a school as socially organized makes it easier for participants to recognize that its energy comes from their interactions and is the system. The inclusion of everything and everybody creates a mindset of belonging and having value instead of being excluded through the "either-or" view. The main social organizing patterns of the school and its leadership consist of formal and informal structures of networks, self-organization, and collaboration.

Organizational charts show the formal organizing processes and structures that distribute official power in the system. The school and leaders' informal structures and processes form the social networks, created by individuals working together and spreading power among the stakeholders. In the QSSL paradigm, most individuals are in the followers' group forming the informal networks that are the heart and spirit of the school. The leader's power to create a new base for thinking and a new culture of everybody working together occurs by accessing the networks' communication chains and the web of networks, especially the informal ones.

Stakeholders describe their school as having a unique culture and personality, portraying it with human characteristics to create its meaningfulness for them. Using human descriptions creates a feeling of aliveness about the school, which helps people understand the change process by connecting it more easily to life processes. In leadership and a school, relating to life processes, socially and biologically, makes it easier to recognize how people react, communicate, and act during change (Tsao & Laszlo, 2019).

Leaders and followers use a living system's natural processes and behaviors, such as networking and self-organizing, to produce information and meaning to respond effectively and proactively to the environment. This life-centered view of schools shifts the perspective to one of connectedness, emphasi*zing how to organize people to work together*, transforming the *way people work together* (Wheatley, 2017). A quantum leader distributes power by influencing a critical mass of participants to develop new thinking patterns on how one feels about accessing, constructing, and using knowledge. Shared knowledge is shared power that makes a difference!

Lead with Soul Overview

The heartbeat of leadership comes from the soul and spirit of individuals. The heart, not the head, is the school's emotional energy source for motivation, buy-in, loyalty, and the needed connectedness to others. The leader's work occurs in a socially constructed world that thrives on the emotional space within relationships, the white space of leadership. Leadership instills a positive life orientation in all aspects of their work by actively affirming positive behaviors through mentoring, coaching, and promoting individual development.

The leader develops the ability and desire in others to participate in leadership individually and collectively by encouraging knowledge expansion and developing the individual's leadership mindset, abilities, and skill sets to be intentional and informed participants. By being highly self-aware, the mindset focuses on constantly connecting to purpose and aligning oneself to others, the organization, and beyond (Tsao & Laszlo, 2019).

QSSL creates a remarkable combination of individual and collective thinking, accessing all the potential for learning, influencing, and acting to develop the processes, relationships, and work structures important for generating adaptive school change. Every day, every moment, the strategic leader models ethical and principled behavior in their work by being compassionate, caring, passionate, courageous, and authentic.

The bedrock of the leader is in ethics and integrity for leading with conviction and principles to move others to trust them and join them (Bolman & Deal, 1995). Values and beliefs are lived daily, showing that these are not just empty words. The quantum strategic leader's actions speak louder than words by *talking the talk* and *walking the walk* for quantum strategic leaders believe their work is a *calling, not just a job*.

CALL TO ACTION

Quantum strategic school leadership calls for individuals to courageously step forward to awaken in others the belief that everyone's participation and leadership are needed to create and sustain positive schooling for students to prosper in the present while preparing for an unknown future. Leaders are invited to embrace QSSL as the unifying force for knowing how to use the full potential for thinking, creating, belonging, energizing, and learning to promote sustainable positive change for the individual, the collective, the organization, and the earth.

QSSL provides ideas for recognizing behaviors, processes, and structures suited to leading, working, and living in an interdependent organization in a networked world. The framework suggests ways to learn, practice, and reflect on leadership that can make a difference. QSSL is more than leadership for change; it ultimately establishes a different worldview and mindset for a way of thinking and acting for living and working powerfully in complex times. The call to action is for schools to use quantum strategic school leadership to guide others to foster sustainability for students, the organization, the individual, society, and the planet.

REFERENCES

Bennis, W. G. (1989). *On becoming a leader*. Addison-Wesley Pub. Co.
Bolman, L., & Deal, T. (1995). *Leading with soul*. Jossey-Bass Inc.
Capra, F., & Luisi, P. (2014). *The systems view of life: A unifying vision*. Cambridge University Press.
Daft, R. L., & Lengel, R. H. (1998). *Fusion leadership: Unlocking subtle forces of people and organizations*. Berrett-Koehler.
Elkington, R., Steege, M., Glick-Smith, J., & Breen, J. M. (2017). *Visionary leadership in a turbulent world: Thriving in the new VUCA context*. Emerald Publishing.
Laszlo, K. (2012). From systems thinking to systems being: The embodiment of evolutionary leadership. *Journal of Organizational Transformation & Social Change, 9*, 95–108.
Obolensky, N. (2010). *Complex adaptive leadership: Embracing paradox and uncertainty*. Ashgate.
Snyder, K. J., Acker-Hocevar, M., & Snyder, K. M. (2000, 2008). *Living on the edge of chaos: Leading schools into the global age*. ASQ Quality Press.
Tsao, F. C., & Laszlo, C. (2019). *Quantum leadership: New consciousness in business*. Stanford Business Books.
Wheatley, M. J. (2017). *Who do we choose to be?* Berrett-Koehler.
Zohar, D. (1997). *Rewiring the corporate brain: Using the new science to rethink how we structure and lead organizations*. Berrett-Koehler.
Zohar, D. (2016). *The quantum leader: A revolution in business thinking and practice*. Prometheus Books.

Chapter Five

Networking for Principal Sustainability

A Chapter of Hope

David Scanga and Renee Sedlack

There is a crisis looming in school leadership that has implications for the sustainability of schooling. According to a recent study by the National Association of Secondary School Principals (NASSP), there is a mass exodus of principals ahead. The study, which surveyed a nationally representative pool of school principals in the United States, showed a predicted fragile rate of principal retention as well as a fractured pipeline of aspiring leaders (NASSP, 2022).

Issues such as accountability, school safety, and violence, the rise of mental health issues in both staff and students, the influence of social media, and the shortage of qualified applicants for vacant positions have made the principalship less attractive to potential candidates and affected the rate of retention of those already in the role.

The issue of principal turnover impacts the stability of schools and the achievement of students. *Fortune* magazine recently labeled America's schools as an endangered institution, highlighting the national concern about the quality of education provided for its youth (Lannon, 2021). It is worthwhile to seek alternatives to the current way of work that has not shown to be productive in enhancing student achievement, providing principals with a pathway to develop a positive school culture, and preventing school leaders from becoming overwhelmed.

In addition, almost half of the principals surveyed by NASSP (2022), reported that the role of the principal has changed significantly because of the coronavirus outbreak. The loss of experienced leaders will have a devasting effect on schooling, especially in communities of poverty, where education is the pathway to more positive life outcomes.

While there may be effective teachers in failing schools, schools cannot be effective without strong leaders (NASSP, 2017). Thus, a discussion about the current shortage of principal candidates is important to understand the underlying causes of the hesitancy of aspiring leaders to seek principalship positions.

This chapter will explore the concepts of systems thinking and related ideas as solutions to principals' struggles to develop schools into places of productivity and positive wellness. Sustainability for quality in education may depend on principals' ability to create natural networks of support. The power to create these networks as a strategy to address the current crisis in principal retention is a realistic solution.

PRINCIPAL RETENTION: A GROWING CRISIS

Principal turnover has the potential to affect the sustainability of schooling. According to the Learning Policy Institute, 18% of principals left their positions in the last year, while in high-poverty schools 21% of principals were no longer at their schools. The findings of a recent research study jointly conducted by the Learning Policy Institute and the National Association of Secondary Principals found that one in six principals leave their school each year and one in five leave in high poverty schools, contributing to the already critical issues of racial and socioeconomic disparities in education (Bradley & Levin, 2019).

Alarming as these statistics were a few years ago, recent studies indicate that the situation has worsened in the United States. Job satisfaction is at an all-time low with almost 40% of principals planning to leave the profession within three years, threatening the sustainability of schooling (NASSP, 2022).

Why are principals leaving? The National Association of Secondary School Principals (NASSP) and the Learning Policy Institute (LPI) conducted focus groups to determine the factors that create principal turnover (Levin et al., 2019). The findings from this study and similar studies suggest five reasons principals leave their jobs: inadequate preparation and ongoing support, poor working conditions that lead to stress and burnout, insufficient salaries, lack of autonomy, and ineffective accountability policies (Beausaert et al., 2016; Fuller & Young, 2009; Levin et al., 2019).

In addition, concerns about the social and emotional health of students, the lack of adequate resources to address significant issues, the influence of political pressure on decision making, and the increasing trend of micromanagement and intervention are issues that have increased the already stressful nature of such a position of responsibility (Washington, 2021). The coronavirus pandemic added concerns about staff and student wellness, as well as personal and family health and implementing mandates and procedures in a politically charged nation (NASSP, 2022).

In a study of 12 principals who had voluntarily left their positions, it was discovered that there were common themes among those included in the study, all of whom had at least 10 years on the job. Issues of school culture, facilitating change among resistant staff, unrealistic and increasing workloads, bureaucracy on multiple levels, student discipline, and unsupportive and hostile parents contributed to the decision to leave the principalship (Johnson, 2005).

These negative factors are barriers to productive work that lead to school improvement including coherent instructional practices, professional capacity of staff, strong parent-community-school ties, team structures, and managing systems of safety, finance, and compliance (Bryk et al., 2015).

A list of concerns from novice principals included workload and task management, daily conflict resolution, curriculum and instruction issues, reform initiatives, lack of resources, and accountability pressures (Beam et al., 2016). The life of a newly appointed principal often comes with feelings of being overwhelmed, underappreciated, and alone. School districts are seeking ways to develop a talent pipeline to address the shortage of school leaders.

The effects of principal turnover are significant as described in a Brown University working paper (Henry & Harbatkin, 2019). The influence of principal turnover affects a variety of school outcomes, including lower test scores and teacher retention. In an examination of administrative data from North Carolina, the authors describe a multi-year decline in student achievement and the inability to retain teachers during the first three years after a principal's departure.

Complicating the need for school principals is the current teacher shortage in the United States. Since teachers make up the largest pool of principal applicants, it is imperative to have a qualified pool of aspiring leaders. In a recent survey of almost 1,200 school districts, two-thirds responded that they had a teacher shortage, with the greatest need being in urban schools (Buttner, 2021). With colleges of education graduating fewer educators, this issue is concerning. In 2022, the State of Florida reported a grim picture of the teacher shortage with almost 5,000 vacancies, especially in classes for special needs students (Daily, 2022).

CHALLENGES FOR PRINCIPALS

School leadership is second to classroom instruction in influencing student achievement (NASSP, 2022). Support for principals in terms of professional development, training, and mentoring has been lacking. Coaching in instructional leadership practices and attention to emotional and physical health have been absent as strategies to make the principalship more manageable (NASSP, 2022).

While principals enjoyed the aspects of their role as providing hope and support for their students, their concerns centered around the lack of decision-making authority and accountability systems that often do not support continuous academic growth. The challenge of maintaining a healthy work-life balance and motivation as a leader while juggling government mandates that often lack alignment with their vision were also factors that contributed to increased frustration with their ability to be influential leaders (Levin et al., 2019).

The role and responsibilities of the principal have changed significantly. Those in the position are finding they are increasingly frustrated and stressed (Fullan, 2014). Let's examine strategies for a new vision and way of work for school principals today, exploring opportunities for the sustainability of schooling.

SYSTEMS THINKING PERSPECTIVE

Systems thinking is a way for educational leaders to understand and manage the complexity and interconnectedness of the school organization (Garland et al., 2018). It shifts the principal's focus to sustaining the school's ability to develop a culture of optimism and capacity building for school improvement. Capra and Luisi (2014) make a case for networks as the core structure of systems that create and sustain the culture.

Attending to networks is crucial to how the system achieves its vision, adapts to changes in the environment, and sustains a positive work culture. Snyder et al. (2008) emphasize that networking has become a primary leadership skill for the global age.

Networks are a fundamental unit of all living things (Capra, 2007; Slaughter, 2017; Snyder et al., 2008). Every living thing is in some way networked with other living things. Whether considering a single cell, a complex being, or a social group, connections exist both internally and externally that help sustain the life of the organism or social unit. In a social setting, such as a school, networks flourish in various forms, both formal and informal, large and small, tightly bonded or loosely connected. The patterns of social relations within the organization make up the network.

We can study these network patterns from a perspective of quantity and quality. Why does the network exist? How often do people come together? How many people are connected? Who are the influencers in the group? How strong are the bonds that bind them together? Is there positive or negative energy in the group? What do they produce? All of these questions and more define the purpose and existence of the network. The science of networks is an integral part of systems thinking, and leaders that attend to the science of networks are part of a new global community that seeks positive and sustainable change.

Snyder et al. (2008) emphasize that networking has become a primary leadership skill for the global age. Principals both new and experienced, live in networks, whether or not they choose to acknowledge them. Leaders that are skilled at networking can leverage the network for positive, sustainable growth.

Networking is defined as the leader's ability to connect individuals who will provide support, camaraderie, feedback, insight, resources, and information to the collective members. The idea that a strong alliance with others in a purposeful network will position the leader for success is well established in the literature (Cullen-Lester et al., 2016; Fullan, 2011; Senge et al., 2008; Snyder et al., 2008).

Leaders who are well connected to stakeholders have continual access to information that provides a systemic view of the organization. The leader's co-involvement with networks significantly increases the probability that interactions and decisions will create positive energy and strengthen the organization.

If networking has become a foundational leadership skill for the global age, then we must consider how the skill of networking is developed in leaders. How do leaders, especially novice leaders, develop networks that increase their capacity to lead?

A good place for leaders to start is understanding the mechanics of networks so that they can take advantage of the positive energy networks create. Luhmann (in Capra & Luisi, 2014) and Capra (2007) wrote extensively on applying what is known about networks in systems theory to social systems like families, schools, and communities. The energy that binds a social network together is not the physical ties of the biological world.

In a social system, what binds individuals together is the process of exchanging ideas through communication, influence, and relationships. Principals are in a key position to leverage social networks since they sit at the apex of an organization and have direct access to all stakeholders. They are, in network terminology, a major hub!

As a major hub in the social network of a school, communication continuously flows to and from the principal. "As communications recur in multiple feedback loops, they produce a shared system of beliefs, explanations, and values—a common context of meaning" (Capra & Luisi, 2014, p. 308). It is communication that creates and sustains the links and bonds of a network. Think of communication as analogous to our body's circulation system. The flow of blood between all parts of the body is an exchange of life-giving oxygen.

Similarly, the exchange of information through communication creates ideas, shared beliefs, expectations, ways of work, and purpose in the social network of people. The energy released as communication within the network keeps the network viable, changing, and self-generating in adaption to the current context of its existence. Communication throughout the system produces changes in beliefs, thinking, and behavior, and thus contributes to the network's way of work.

Principals, seasoned and novice, may or may not be cognizant of the potential of leveraging networks to enhance their leadership and leadership within the school. The idea of networking as a leadership skill is relatively new and requires some intentionality to develop. Now more than ever leaders need to become part of a global network society that strives for the sustainability of educational systems driven by what we truly believe is the purpose of education.

PRINCIPAL SUSTAINABILITY THROUGH PURPOSEFUL NETWORKS

Principal turnover and mobility, in part, result from feeling isolated and overwhelmed by heavy responsibility. Being a leader means working with and through others, and there is no better way than using systems thinking and networks to accomplish the goals of the organization. Leadership is enhanced when networks are recognized as a basic pattern of living in an organization (Capra & Luisi, 2014; Snyder & Snyder, 2021).

Everything and everyone are connected in an interdependent web of interactions. Networks, with vital links to other leaders inside and outside of the school organization, are one way to sustain young leaders in positions, counteracting the negative pressures of factors such as ineffective accountability measures, the focus on management issues, and the daily resolution of conflict with stakeholders.

Developing the leadership ability to build and use networks, starts with a mindset that there is power in our connections to others—a network mindset. A network mindset begins with leaders accepting that meaningful change can only be accomplished by working with others in a team atmosphere. Working in isolation has virtually disappeared in today's complex school environment (Snyder & Snyder, 2021). A network of networks facilitates and directs all the work. Networks afford us the ability to engage with others in ways that create excitement and interest (Capra & Luisi, 2014).

The leadership skill of building a network requires a new mindset that is tuned to notice who can make decisions, execute plans, influence others, accomplish goals in time, and access resources. People have different kinds of power and strengths—knowing this is helpful. A network mindset invests in creating an integrated system of networks that complement and self-generate energy to "drive the work culture toward a common vision and mission" (Snyder et al., 2008, p. 251).

The story that follows captures the power of networks in addressing what has become a crisis of recruitment and retention in educational leadership. Developing leadership skills in building and utilizing networks is a critical component of sustaining systems in schools that address today's complex challenges.

ONE STORY: A NETWORK FOR NOVICE PRINCIPALS

The problem of principal recruitment and retention is occurring across the globe, and a systemic change is needed if we hope to have sustainable opportunities for all children to succeed in education. Judith Chapman (2005), in a UNESCO report condensing years of best practices, stated that the loss of school leadership has a direct adverse effect on the quality of the student learning environment. Often a change in school leadership is a disruption in school improvement efforts.

Therefore, the rapid succession of new principals in many school organizations, both nationally and globally, brings to light the need for change. Principals, especially novice principals, frequently express worries about early success and how to balance the stress points between opportunities and vulnerabilities. There is always a fear of failure, or at the very least, of disappointing the organization after being entrusted with the new principal role. These feelings of anxiety have resulted in early retirements, changes in positions, and even changes to a different profession.

Principals express a need for additional, and different kinds of support. Typical support structures for new principals are often driven by top-down initiatives (Chapman, 2005; Snyder, 2015). Centralized support structures for new leaders include direct supervision, district meetings, and the typical departmental connections, all based on vertical communication. What appears to be lacking is the less structured, horizontal development and support connecting school leaders across the organization, particularly within a cadre of others who are new to the role.

A community for learning is needed, a grassroots movement, working with others who face the same challenges and pressures of overseeing a school.

Networking with other novice principals is a valuable prototype of professional support explored in this story of a group of novice principals looking for ways to survive as leaders in challenging times. Research supports the notion that an informal network of peers reinforces learning and provides emotional support (Bryk et al., 2015; Chitpin, 2014; Slaughter, 2017; Snyder & Snyder, 2021).

The combination of both hierarchical and horizontal support provides leaders with a holistic, collaborative environment where positive connections allow for camaraderie, professional learning, and sustainability of the organization's culture.

The story of the New Elementary Principal Network (NEPN), an innovative initiative in a central Florida school district, began with an assistant superintendent who recognized the overwhelming challenges facing newly inducted principals who are navigating the complexities of leading schools. New principals are known to say, "I had no idea it would be this tough." No one seems able to anticipate the level of responsibility, communication, and workload until they are in the position.

The NEPN was designed as a network prototype to give novice principals an environment to foster trust, respect, and belonging, and a safe place to reflect, collaborate, and learn from each other. The NEPN evolved to fill a natural gap addressing the need to create sustainable professional development and enhance principals' self-efficacy who have accepted the position despite the many challenges. The district support, while helpful, was not enough to address the complexity of the work undertaken by new principals.

District supports are not frequent enough or at the right intensity to provide timely information and assurances that principals need. A network of peers, based on what we know about network science, was explored to expand opportunities for connecting with other principals in a professional learning network.

Chitpin (2014) supports this idea of networking by pointing out that principals face two barriers in today's fast-paced, demanding school setting. A principal's work is fragmented, with attention being given, sometimes in quick succession, to various stakeholders: parents, students, teachers, community members, and the district. This makes the microcosm of the school community feel very isolating at times, something a network of peers can address.

Chitpin's (2014) other barrier is the limited support from a school district for their professional learning. Typical support is usually focused on management and compliance with a set agenda determined by the principals' supervisors. The NEPN was designed around network thinking to create a space for collaboration, problem solving, and growth through personal relationships with others living a similar professional life.

Observations and data from the New Elementary Principals Network (NEPN) participants indicate that networks of new principals often comprised only a few personal friends from previous schools and a small number of district personnel. While these limited ties may be strong, they do not seem to counteract the feelings of being overwhelmed, isolated, and vulnerable in the new role as principal. When asked about a key take-away one member wrote, "The importance of each other and carving out time to process with each other. It can be a very lonely job if you don't."

Expansive networks provide depth and diversity of ideas and a feeling of belonging to a community, both elements new principals say are needed in their efforts to succeed. Having access to a more extensive, more diverse professional learning network provides the ongoing learning and support needed to help new leaders flourish.

The story of the New Elementary Principal Network was driven by a need to not only retain principals in school leadership but also build the sustainability of schools that are going through dramatic change. The assistant superintendent saw the potential that network thinking had as a strategy to foster positive energy, resiliency, and engagement among the 12 elementary principals, all having less than three years of experience as principals. The demographics of the schools led by the 12 principals varied in several variables, including socioeconomics, size, racial diversity, rural versus suburban, and achievement levels.

Despite differences in school communities, the principals frequently expressed having the same leadership concerns and problems as their colleagues. One principal wrote, "We are all going through similar experiences, and it will be helpful to be able to talk with and collaborate with others." Another principal wrote, "Jenny's story helped me feel not so alone and gave me ideas on how to approach similar situations."

What worked for the NEPN participants was a strong feeling of connectedness and empowerment to drive the agenda and co-construct learning based on their experiences and needs. The NEPN goals included nurturing relationships between the participants and giving them a venue for professional development and common problem solving.

The formation of an informal network, like the New Elementary Principal Network (NEPN), is a process that moves through stages. At first, the facilitators needed to guide and encourage participation in the network, but ultimately, the members owned the network. The intentional design of the NEPN included structures and routines that would encourage individuals to develop valuable, meaningful, and productive relationships within a network of peers. Examples of conventions used in the NEPN include the following:

1. Group norms and routines for sharing ideas helped principals build trust in expectations between individuals and the group.
2. Strengths of individuals were studied using the Clifton Strengths Finder (Gallup) survey.
3. Exposure to professional literature gave the group a sense of building knowledge around critical issues in education.
4. A leadership platform was written that expressed beliefs, values, and attitudes that are the foundation of the leader's practice.
5. Problems of practice are a routine that allows members to discuss and get feedback from peers on a specific issue or problem they face.
6. Celebrations were shared among members to strengthen personal connections.

Networks depend on trust (Clark, 2020; Slaughter, 2017). The routines and structure of the NEPN built a safe environment that created inclusivity and the development of deep relational trust among members. Individuals in the group felt a sense of community and shared purpose. There was a high level of personal safety resulting from social acceptance and a lack of judgment. Belongingness, paramount to a functional network, was evident in the unquestionable acceptance of each person's strengths and weaknesses.

Being vulnerable, and admitting a lack of knowledge or understanding, was a normal part of the dialogue. Group norms and procedures strengthen connections and create safety. The code of the group was acceptance and confidentiality. The group norms reviewed at the start of every meeting included solution-focused commitment to connecting personally, thoughts and ideas staying confidential, leveraging our strengths, providing empathy (space for each to "just" share), and offering grace for each other and ourselves. The NEPN norms reflect a commitment to unconditional acceptance and trust.

As the safe environment of the NEPN unfolded, the members showed a high interest in discovery, taking risks, and asking questions, all behaviors indicative of strong networks (Clark, 2020; Snyder & Snyder, 2021). Principals are highly motivated to learn. They seek value in the time spent together. The principals expressed a need for camaraderie and emotional support and focused on collaborative problem solving and learning from one another. The structure of the time spent together and the repetition of routines was purposeful in creating a safe learning space.

For example, the "problems of practice exercise" gave voice to personal challenges in a nonjudgmental space, knowing that clarifying questions would help the presenter think deeper about possible solutions or ways to act. Routines, whether a celebration or problem solving, require active engagement in processes of co-constructing meaning within a secure network of like-minded friends. A learner benefits from intimacy and accountability in a dynamic network of professional relationships.

Leaders, by nature, want to make a difference in their lives and the lives of others. Contributors add value to the discussion and actions of the group. The NEPN became a very active, engaged cohort. The value added by individuals might stem from experience, expertise, positive disposition, or being an active listener. As relationships deepen, competencies emerge to strengthen the links between participants resulting in a common understanding of how each individual contributes to the network.

The willingness to contribute showed up around the third meeting when NEPN members began volunteering ideas and providing direction based on feedback collected at the end of each session. An established "Ticket Out the Door" survey provided input on what was working and what needed to be considered. For example, comments from the third NEPN meeting asked for more time to solve problems and discuss hot topics. Hot topics later became another routine of the group.

Throughout the first year, the NEPN continued to adapt and change, but what became apparent was the ownership of the network. The bonds between principals strengthened to the point that communication occurred ongoing, and members used a group text for daily problem solving. The monthly meetings became an anticipated event to come together for learning and support. Principals now had a sustainable system that thrived on inquisitive questions, problem solving, and shared solutions.

The NEPN became a place to share ideas and get different perspectives on common and sometimes not so common problems. Trusted relationships formed that led to a strong collaborative effort to sustain leadership through the energy of networks. The intended organic nature of the network empowered the principals, and by the end of the school year, a charge of energy was felt in the group.

They were networked—working together, sharing ideas, developing group projects, emboldened to take control of their story as they continue to grow as young leaders. As one participant wrote, "The time spent with this group will have a lasting impact on me. Thank you for this opportunity and the support you have provided throughout while still growing me as a leader!" The New Elementary Principal Network became a prototype of a systems thinking approach to promote sustainability in education.

CALL TO ACTION

Continued sustainable schooling will depend on strong, healthy leaders. While school principals today are facing challenges and obstacles to their ability to lead in ways that build nurturing and high performing places to teach and learn, it is well established that principal sustainability may be enhanced through purposeful networks, a structure of relationships, and partnerships to collaborate for a shared vision and focused work, and a mindset that through supportive networks, principals can lead in positive ways.

The New Elementary Principal Network is one example of a system of support that is easily replicated to provide psychological safety and generate positive energy for principals to enjoy the personal satisfaction and joy once again in being school leaders.

How can your school system create natural networks of collaboration, energy, and support? How can you channel positive energy to ignite change? This is a call to action for school systems around the world to rise to the challenge of seeking innovative ways to support both novice and experienced school leaders in ways to enhance principal sustainability. Meet the challenge with a promise for a new way of work.

REFERENCES

Bartanen, B., Grissom, J., & Rogers, L. (2019). The impacts of principal turnover. *Educational Evaluation and Policy Analysis*, *41*(3), 350–374. https://doi.org/10.3102/0162373719855044

Beam, A., Claxton, R. L., & Smith, S. J. (2016). Challenges for novice school leaders: Facing today's issues in school administration. *Educational Leadership and Administration*, *27*, 145–162. https://digitalcommons.liberty.edu/educ_fac_pubs/233

Beausaert, S., Froehlich, B., Devos, C., & Riley, P. (2016). Effects of support on stress and burnout in school principals. *Educational Research*, *58*(4), 347–365. https://doi.org/10.1080/00131881.2016.1220810

Bradley, K., & Levin, S. (2019). Understanding and addressing principal turnover. *National Association of Secondary School Principals*. https://www.nassp.org/2019/06/05/understanding-and-addressing-principal-turnover/

Bryk, A. S., Gomez, L. M., Grunow, A., & LeMahieu, P. G. (2015). *Learning to improve: How America's schools can get better at getting better*. Harvard Education Press.

Buttner, A. (2021). The teacher shortage, 2021 edition. *Frontline Education*. https://www.frontlineeducation.com/blog/teacher-shortage-2021/

Capra, F. (2007). Complexity and life. *Systems Research and Behavioral Science*, *24*(5), 475–479. https://doi.org/10.1002/sres.848

Capra, F., & Luisi, P. L. (2014). *The systems view of life: A unifying vision.* Cambridge University Press.

Chapman, J. (2005). Recruitment, retention, and development of school principals. *International Academy of Education and the International Institute for Educational Planning.* https://unesdoc.unesco.org/ark:/48223/pf0000140987

Chitpin, S. (2014). Principals and the professional learning community: Learning to mobilize knowledge. *International Journal of Education Management, 28*(2), 215–229.

Clark, T. (2020). *The 4 stages of psychological safety: Defining the path to inclusion and innovation.* Berrett-Koehler Publishers.

Cullen-Lester, K. L., Woehler, M. L., & Willburn, P. (2016). Network-based leadership development: A guiding framework and resources for management educators. *Journal of Management Education, 40*(3), 1–38. https://doi.org/10.1177/1052562915624124

Daily, R. (2022). A report paints a grim picture of Florida's teacher shortage. *WUSF Public Media.* https://wusfnews.wusf.usf.edu/education/2022-02-09/a-report-paints-a-grim-picture-about-floridas-critical-teacher-shortage

Fullan, M. (2011). *Change leadership: Learning to do what matters.* Jossey-Bass Publishers.

Fullan, M. (2014). *The principal: Three keys to maximizing impact.* Jossey-Bass Publishers.

Fuller, E., & Young, M. (2009). Tenure and retention of newly hired principals in Texas. *University Council for Education Administration.* https://www.casciac.org/pdfs/ucea_tenure_and_retention_report_10_8_09.pdf

Garland, J., Layland, A., & Corbett, J. (2018). Systems thinking leadership for district and school improvement. *Illinois Center for School Improvement at American Institute for Research.* http://www.corbetteducation.com/ILCSI_Improvement Systems_June18.pdf

Henry, G. T., & Harbatkin, E. (2019). Turnover at the top: Estimating the effects of principal turnover on student, teacher, and school outcomes. (EdWorkingPaper: 19–95). *Annenberg Institute at Brown University.* https://doi.org/10.26300/c7m1-bb67

Johnson, L. A. (2005). Why principals quit. *Principal.* http://www.naesp.org/sites/default/files/resources/2/Principal/2005/J-Fp21.pdf

Kominiak, T. (2018). The changing role of the school principal. *TrustED K-12 Insights.* https://www.k12insight.com/trusted/changing-role-school-principal-2/

Lannon, C. (2021). Revitalizing the schools: A system's thinking approach. *Systems Thinker.* https://thesystemsthinker.com/revitalizing-the-schools-a-systems-thinking-approach/

Levin, S., Bradley, K., & Scott, C. (2019). Principal turnover: Insights from current principals. *National Association of Secondary School Principals* (NASSP). https://learningpolicyinstitute.org/product/nassp-principal-turnover-insights-brief

Levin, S., Scott, C., Yang, M., Leung, M., & Bradley, K. (2020). Supporting a strong stable principal workforce: What matters and what can be done. *Learning*

Policy Institute. https://learningpolicyinstitute.org/product/supporting-strong-stable-principal-workforce-report

National Association of Secondary School Principals (NASSP). (2017). Principal statement: Principal shortage. *Policy and Advocacy Center.* https://www.nassp.org/wp-content/uploads/2020/06/Principal_Shortage.pdf

National Association of Secondary School Principals (NASSP). (2022). NASSP survey signals a looming mass exodus of principals from schools. https://www.nassp.org/news/nassp-survey-signals-a-looming-mass-exodus-of-principals-from-schools/

Rangel, V. S. (2018). A review of the literature on principal turnover. *Review of Educational Research, 88*(1), 87–124. https://doi.org/10.3102/0034654317743197

Senge, P., Smith, B., Kruschhwitz, N., Laur, J., & Schley, S. (2008). *The necessary revolution: How individuals and organizations are working together to create a sustainable world.* Doubleday Publishing Group.

Slaughter, A. (2017). *The chessboard and the web: Strategies of connection in a networked world.* Yale University Press.

Snyder, K. J., Acker-Hocevar, M., & Snyder, K. M. (2008). *Living on the edge of chaos: Leading schools into the global age* (2nd ed.). American Society for Quality, Quality Press.

Snyder, K. J., & Snyder, K. M. (2021). The role of human network systems for leading sustainable quality in organizations. In *Proceedings of the 27th Annual Conference International Sustainable Development Research Society*, Mid Sweden University. Östersund.

Snyder, K. M. (2015). Engaging leaders develop schools as quality organizations. *International Journal of Quality and Service Sciences, 7*(2/3), 217–229.

Superville, D. (2019). Principal turnover is a problem: New data helps districts combat it. *Education Weekly.* https://www.edweek.org/leadership/principal-turnover-is-a-problem-new-data-could-help-districts-combat-it/2019/12

Taie, S., & Goldring, R. (2017). Characteristics of public elementary and secondary school principals in the United States: Results from the 2015–16 national teacher and principal survey. *U.S. Department of Education*: National Center for Education Statistics. https://nces.ed.gov/pubsearch/pubsinfo.asp?pubid=2017070

Troyer, M. (2019). 25 ways American education has changed in the last decade. *Stacker.* https://stacker.com/stories/3665/25-ways-american-education-has-changed-last-decade

Washington, C. (2021). I saved myself: Five reasons why principals leave their schools. *The Educators Room.* https://theeducatorsroom.com/i-saved-myself-five-reasons-why-principals-leave-their-schools/

Chapter Six

The Beginnings of Collaboration in Schools

Team Teaching and Multi-Age Grouping

Robert H. Anderson

INTRODUCTION

Over the last seventy years, team teaching has gradually become an active organizational structure in schools, promoted initially by the faculty at Harvard University's School of Education in the 1950s and 1960s, where Robert H. Anderson was a pioneer in its development. Team teaching was the first alternative to the one-teacher-one-classroom tradition, enabling professionals to have greater flexibility and resources for the learning environment. However, the graded one-teacher-per-classroom tradition continues to dominate practice throughout the world today.

The chapter that follows was written by Robert H. Anderson for Karolyn Snyder's training program called Leadership for Sustainable School Development. The 10 authors of this current book, who call themselves the Systems Thinking Collective, pondered how Anderson's important work on team teaching and multi-aged student grouping might be included in this book, for team teaching was the beginning of successful efforts in our work to lead schools from a systems perspective. With the publisher's permission, Anderson's work is included in this chapter.

At Corbett Preparatory School at IDS, a pre-K-to-eighth-grade independent school in Florida (United States), the current head of school, Nicholas Rodriguez, recently commented that without the school's tradition of teaming for everyone, the innovative work that was required during the recent COVID-19 pandemic would not have been possible, for school-wide agility, spontaneity, and resilience became the new norm for those two years. Corbett Prep began its team teaching and multi-aged student grouping practice over 25 years ago under Joyce Swarzman's leadership, which has enabled the school to become one of the most innovative, agile, and responsive schools in the region, and which has led to numerous achievements and recognitions every year for students at all ages.

—Karolyn J. Snyder and Joyce B. Swarzman

What follows in this paper is a summary of changes that have been made over several centuries in the operational dimensions of public schooling. In this review, I draw upon work that I have done within the several major roles that I occupied over many years and my experiences in working professionally in all 50 American states as well as American-oriented schools in 29 countries. In 20 countries I also occasionally worked with government officials and local educators. Most of the work that I did, in all these roles, was related to matters of administration, especially as related to organizational practices and also to help with dimensions of curriculum.

The focus of this brief essay includes nongradedness, team teaching, deliberate use of multi-age classroom instruction and organization, and other deviations from the literally graded patterns that prevailed in American schools (and doubtless schools in other countries, notably European) for more than l00 years after the influential Quincy Grammar School was founded in Boston in 1848. The Quincy pattern was rigidly graded, and it was based upon the then-accepted (although inaccurate) belief that children of approximately the same age (within a 12-month period) could efficiently be offered the same curriculum. Also, unfortunately, there were related assumptions about the probable resistance of virtually all children to productive and compliant school behaviors. Therefore, it took many years before an atmosphere encouraging healthy, productive, and noncompetitive interaction began to be observable in classrooms. It also took a long time before practices such as extensive whole-class instruction, the use of rigidly defined measurement and evaluation systems, and other examples of austerity began to be modified.

Much educational history in America, and probably in Europe (and other places) as well, began centuries ago, and probably on both continents the original goal was not particularly related to mass publicly supported schooling. In America, in what was called dame schools in the 17th century and in the so-called district schools of the 18th century, as was also the case in most medical practices, there were few if any theoretical underpinnings. Instruction was nearly always provided by untrained and often less-than-effective teachers. The teaching pattern was, of necessity, apparently individualized, but the primitive, even crude, features of these early schools reflected an almost total absence of respect for or confidence in the learners.

For well over a hundred years in early America, the universal provision of schooling opportunities to children emerged as a major objective. In the mid-19th century, a long-persistent pattern of gradedness evolved that was much influenced by both architectural structure (featuring self-contained classrooms) and age-oriented teaching strategies such as those that were used in the Quincy Grammar School in Boston, which was founded in 1848.

THE GRADED SCHOOL AND SELF-CONTAINED TEACHING

When the Quincy Grammar School came into being, the need for a manageable system greatly stimulated the development, over a good many years, of what ultimately became the nearly universal American pattern of graded elementary-school organization. Usually, this separated pupils into age groups whose literal age span were about 365 days, and therefore in each class, there were in fact many significant differences in pupil "readiness." These differences were stubbornly ignored as a standard (and, as we are obliged to note, a thin and moralistic) "curriculum" became official. Teachers, all of whom were females with very limited preparation, were apparently not allowed to work, or even talk, together. Their male supervisors, whose knowledge about child growth and development must also have been extremely limited, maintained tight supervisory control.

The primary-school movement that had been launched in Boston became influential as a model for age-graded groupings, and in some ways led over the next several decades to an enormous nationwide growth of graded elementary schools. Almost all of them featured classrooms of a size intended to accommodate 25–35 pupils who were all expected to function academically within the same "grade" level. In the original Boston school, and probably in most of the schools that came to exist over the ensuing century or more, there continued to be literal self-containment. Nearly all the teachers in the early days of gradedness were young, very poorly educated, and subject to strict supervision. That this rigid situation persisted for a very long time helps to explain why it took the better part of a century for more appropriate patterns to emerge.

Inasmuch as the earliest public schools in the United States were small, a primitive although not necessarily intentional version of what is now identified as multi-age schooling has in fact existed for a long time. By the middle of the 19th century, however, many communities had blossomed into cities with substantial populations, and soon there had emerged buildings large enough to accommodate aggregates of children who could be packaged into classrooms designated for first grade, second grade, and so on. The teachers, nearly all women and nearly all, as noted, with a very rudimentary education, were assigned in each case to one of the graded classes, and over time there evolved a sequential curriculum of sorts.

Of interest to 21st-century educators is that the Quincy architectural layout, a series of similarly sized "boxes" called classrooms, became "fixed" over the next hundred or more years. The pattern of teacher self-containment was universally maintained, despite its severe limitations, and not only elementary-level teacher preparation programs but supervisory models almost always assumed that each teacher was operationally, and probably psychologically, almost totally independent of colleagues, even those in physically adjoining classrooms.

The management arrangements of gradedness, as noted, included assembly in conventionally sized classroom spaces of children whose ages were claimed to be appropriate for each successive grade level. The relative progress of the children was measured through tests and observations, and patterns of retention-in-grade tended to be inflexible and mechanistic. Awareness of the rigidity of the system led, over many decades, to a significant outpouring of theories and proposals for alternative arrangements, which at least during those decades dominated the educational literature, received significant attention of various kinds, and stimulated a great many architectural and organizational adaptations.

There were several reasons, all regrettable when viewed a century or more later, for the fixation that supported the pattern of classroom self-containment and the accompanying suspicion of the motives and the intellectual capabilities of children. Not only teachers but physicians, healthcare workers, and others entrusted with the well-being and development of future adults also had lower status many years ago than they have in today's (i.e., 21st-century) world. However, of the groups mentioned, only school workers have remained at the financial mercy of their clients, probably because the financial support of excellent and currently up-to-date schooling (for all children, in every stratum of the society) would in many respects be significantly unaffordable from the taxpayers' viewpoint. Also, it seems important to note at this point that definitions of acceptable professional practice and the sufficiency of training of school workers have lagged very, very far behind the levels that obtain in comparable work settings.

The enormous size and the universality of public education have complicated the problem of updating professional education. Even in the 21st century, it seems almost embarrassing to admit that there are few training programs for educators that are even a fraction as demanding and efficacious as those required for other categories of workers for whom the adjective "professional" seems appropriate. The situation is worsened by the calamitous shortage of appropriate candidates for teaching positions.

An accompanying phenomenon has been the powerfully influential system of "standardized" curriculum tests, which by the recent onset of the 21st century had become much entrenched in practice and legally so that in effect the schools and school leadership were becoming highly structured and the flexibility that nongraded practices had been seeking to provide was rapidly disappearing. Goodlad and I, in our 1959 book titled *The Nongraded Elementary School*, acknowledged that gradedness never had any operational validity, although the notion of arbitrarily selecting progressively more advanced materials for each successive graded class did, over time, influence curriculum (and teaching) decisions.

TEAM TEACHING

Among the extremely promising changes that were being made in the mid-20th century, or at least receiving widespread attention, was and probably remains the concept and practice of team teaching. However, in this early decade of the 21st century, children in American schools (more than those in Europe and elsewhere) are suffering from an achievement-testing mania and from a breakdown within the American culture of multi-aged and individually determined progress programs that derive from a commitment to nongradedness. The challenge to educational leaders everywhere, as well as to their overseas counterparts, is to at least soften the influence of the aforementioned mania and to regain and strengthen those attitudes and behaviors that recognize both the existence and the legitimacy of variety in the learning styles and (over the long run) in the personal career goals of children. One style, one learning pattern, and one way of defining child growth and development can no longer be accepted in schools, and in fact in the societies of the world.

Teaming was introduced and soon became, at least in several hundreds of venturesome school districts, a valued alternative to self-containment. As noted above, the latter was an arrangement inherited from centuries-old architectural and operational patterns. These were geared to mostly indefensible assumptions about children's learning needs, motivations, and capabilities. Also deeply entrenched, even though most of them are anomalous given what is now known about human potential, are the prevailing instructional and administrative arrangements. Even though there are full-fledged team-teaching practices in many places, and even though the literally self-contained classroom is now less predominant given some of the ways that teachers find to exchange pupils and share in teaching activities, teacher-preparation programs in nearly all universities continue to assume that their students will mostly be employed to work within the obsolescent pattern of self-containment.

Although in many situations throughout educational history there have been some admirable efforts by teachers to work together and share responsibilities, self-containment was long regarded as a desideratum within teaching. When in the mid-l950s proposals to facilitate teamwork and colleagueship were first announced and then pursued, there was mostly a huge outcry from many educational workers but also a great deal of enthusiasm expressed by those teachers and administrators who elected to become involved in teaming efforts. Unfortunately, the original publications about teaming were mostly geared not only to the virtues of a partnership but also to the concept, which soon met with almost unanimous rejection, especially by teacher unions, of hierarchical staffing patterns. One healthy consequence of the early experimentation with teaming was that it became common for (usually four to six) teachers to work with multi-age (or multigrade) groups of children. This facilitated, or at least stimulated, experimentation with deliberate multi-age pupil groups, and consequently stimulated the abandonment or softening of literal gradedness. Another "bonus" was that, within the larger pupil membership, it became easier (or at least more likely) to implement what in parts of Europe was already known as "family grouping."

Team teaching, which refers to the deliberate formation of arrangements that enable and encourage teachers to work together and to share responsibilities, has taken many forms over the years. It might interest readers to know that over at least a century, there had been many examples of teachers helping and working with each other, for example, in developing new curriculum approaches and sometimes through joining the children in their separate classes for a program or equivalent activity. However, until about 50 or so years ago, there were few if any instances of literal team arrangements. One-room schools, of course, almost always served pupils of mixed ages, and graded structure dominated the atmosphere even though many if not most teachers worked out lesson plans that called for, or permitted, pupils of adjoining ages to work together at least part of the time on topics that enabled mixed-age groups to function.

In the early years of experimentation with patterns of team teaching, Harvard's dean Francis Keppel, who with Francis Chase of Chicago, envisioned the original arrangement, conceptualized teaming as a hierarchical arrangement. In this plan, a typical team would consist of one teacher of outstanding talent who could become the team leader and receive a substantially large salary supplement, and another excellent teacher who could function as an assistant leader at perhaps 40%–50% of the leader's salary supplement, one or more "regularly reimbursed" teachers, and several nonprofessionals. The latter were not certified nor necessarily college graduates, but they usually had good credentials and could be employed at salary levels that were respectable but a significant notch below those of certified teachers. For a typically sized team, therefore, it was expected that the overall salary cost would be essentially equal to the cost of having the same number of adults at "regular" teachers' salaries. Among the arguments for such an arrangement were that fewer credentialed teachers would be required, it would become possible to reward truly outstanding teachers in ways that could enable them to remain working with children, and it would reduce the painstaking workload from teachers.

Several major discoveries or at least serious proposals about better ways to organize elementary and middle schools were made in the United States, beginning in approximately the middle of the 20th century. These led, over several decades, to a significant outpouring of theories and trial arrangements, which at least during those decades dominated the educational literature, received significant attention of various kinds, and stimulated a great many architectural and organizational adaptations.

Team teaching, at least in the introductory period, grew rapidly in acceptance and popularity. It did not take long, however, for arguments to erupt in defense of self-contained classrooms. Yet, thanks to generous financial support from several foundations, along with architectural inventiveness, collaborative arrangements continued to develop and prosper. Furthermore, supported by positive involvement on the part of participating teacher groups, enthusiastic administrators with the enlightened support of their school boards soon created considerable support for and, significantly, sufficient research justification for teaming, which emerged as such arrangements came to be better understood and valued. By the beginning of the next century, however, the almost-universal adoption of teaming that had been predicted had not materialized. Nonetheless, in many schools, it was possible to find that literally self-contained classroom situations no longer existed. Some of the changes that could be detected were architectural (e.g., in connected spaces), but most were found in the multiplicity of collaborative activities that helped teachers and students to expand their contacts beyond the standard classroom.

When the concept of teacher teaming was first explored and developed, in the 1950s, some experienced teachers were resistant, even fearful, because of a presumed loss of privacy and/or independence. In addition, it now seems safe to discuss that such teachers perceived that they would be far less able to function idiosyncratically, even eccentrically, and to skip over or ignore parts of the curriculum that were not easy for them to teach. Even more significantly, it is probably not unfair to note that some teachers find that it is difficult, if not impossible, to deal effectively (and fairly) with all kinds or types of pupils. Many are therefore fearful that working with a much larger group of pupils might expose them to criticism. What came as almost a surprise to many resolutely self-contained teachers was that they had failed to understand or believe that working with several colleagues could and would, almost always, result in the elimination of negatively intended criticism.

Reviewing the impact of forces in American as well as European education, it seems that there is a strong realization that teachers, not separately but as hardworking and talented groups of specialists, must have both an opportunity and an obligation to blend their special talents and interests so that children in their charge can be both better served and more productive of skills and attitudes that will benefit them throughout their working and personal lives. In contrast to the once-accepted roles of teachers as primarily didactic disseminators and pupils as passive beneficiaries, this emerging pair of role definitions should be far more attractive to both the adult staff and their students. The visible and valued aspects of the emerging context would include the following:

1. The deliberate provision of many opportunities for multi-aged and heterogeneous pupil learning experiences.
2. The assembling of teams of teachers whose unique backgrounds and specialized skills are valuable not only to the pupils they serve but also to their adult colleagues/partners.
3. The provision of opportunities, to the extent that it is possible, for parents and community members to become significantly involved in the life of the school.
4. The making of connections, in a variety of ways, with children and teachers from other schools, especially in other countries.

The "professionals" who work in schools almost never have been beneficiaries of professional-quality initial preparation and in-service stimulation. This has always been true; but as many more and better opportunities for well-salaried employment in other jobs became available to those men and (mostly) women who in the past had fewer employment options and therefore became teachers, the job market has changed rather radically.

By the year 2006–2007, it had become virtually impossible for administrators, even in relatively well-financed districts, to staff their schools with significantly well-prepared workers. Placing newly hired "teachers" into groups or clusters influenced in each case by the advice and example of relatively skillful colleagues, sometimes became a helpful approach. A fair amount of "research" was conducted during the first decade or so of teaming, but in retrospect, the research focused too much upon academic progress (which almost always confirmed that at least by well-defined and familiar measures of academic progress the pupils were doing well) and not enough upon the many social and personal-development advantages inherent in team participation.

Suffice to say that in the numerous doctoral studies and faculty inquiries that were made, it had become obvious that the alleged advantages of the self-contained classroom were mostly nonexistent—both for the pupils and for the teachers. Only the fact that many self-contained teachers are and were happy when left alone, plus the regrettable fact that most schools have been (and continue to be) designed with equal-sized classroom boxes, can explain why teaming has not significantly replaced non-collaborative and limited sharing arrangements. Teachers, therefore, remain the only so-called professionals, the majority of whom work mostly by themselves.

By the beginning of the next century, however, the almost-universal adoption of teaming that had been predicted had not materialized. Teaming projects did, nonetheless, exist in many places, and what might be described as an architectural revolution was well underway throughout the country. Also, in a great many schools that did not actually adopt full-fledged teaming practices, it was possible to find that literal self-containment no longer existed. Most changes were found in the multiplicity of collaborative activities that help teachers and students to expand their contacts beyond the standard classroom.

NONGRADEDNESS AND MULTI-AGE GROUPINGS

The second most significant change from "the old days" was symbolized by the increasing use of multi-aged, multitalented, and deliberately heterogeneous pupil groupings. This came about largely because the old and familiar age-oriented pattern of classroom organization was increasingly recognized as both ill-advised and unworkable. The absurdity of dealing with groups of so-called six-year-olds in first grade as if they were all equally ready for "first-grade instruction" as their first school year began was hardly ever acknowledged. For some teachers (and administrators, no doubt), such assumptions provided welcome stability and required hardly any creative and imaginative staff behavior. Even more doubts and suspicions about changing the atmosphere and activities within schools were raised by many parents, who themselves had attended and apparently accepted the aforementioned patterns. Ironically, almost 100% of adults want their doctors, dentists, and other health-oriented workers to be oriented to fully updated medical information. Sadly, to bring schooling equally up to date has been regarded as economically unfeasible, and being at the mercy of taxpayers, school budgets and practices are very rarely if ever, funded at sufficient levels.

John I. Goodlad and I were the first Americans, and probably the first in the world, to write extensively about nongraded (originally called ungraded) elementary schools. Nongradedness was at that time a fairly new topic that had been written about only within the several (mostly Wisconsin and New York) communities that had been "experimenting" prior to 1959 or so, with the abandonment or serious modification of the almost universally prevalent graded school structure. Goodlad and I, who had become friends while working toward PhD degrees at the University of Chicago, discovered that both of us were enthusiastic about the modification of literal gradedness and were also preparing manuscripts that would eventually become stimuli for our co-involvement in a book.

There were a great many efforts at least to soften, if not destroy, the graded school pattern; and in the 20th century, doubtless stimulated by our writings and those of many others, the nongraded pattern of organizing elementary schools came to be quite common, although not universal. Notable was the fact that in the decade prior to the Great Depression, in the 1920s, it was common for American elementary teachers, especially those working in German-oriented cities (such as Milwaukee), to spend their summers studying what it seems appropriate nowadays to label as nongradedness under famous professors such as Peter Peterson in Germany.

Goodlad was the organizer of our effort, and he took the responsibility of seeking a publisher who would be interested in the topic. I remember that it took almost two frustrating years before Harcourt Brace, whose senior editor was Paul Brandwein, agreed to a contract with us. The book appeared in 1959. By then a particularly important and relevant 1957 study examining and advocating deliberate multi-age grouping had come to our attention. We noted the multi-age concept in our book, but it was too late to pay enough attention to it, and we regretted that fact so much that we almost literally forced Harcourt Brace to let us rewrite especially pages 68–78 and issue a "Revised Edition" in 1963 with what we regarded as a significant strengthening. Some readers might be interested in reading the introduction to the 1963 edition (pp. vii and viii) to understand what we did. The publisher was eventually, we think, happy about the revisions that we made; and the unexpected success of our material over the years led to some gratifying national and international recognition.

The very word "grade" is a bit mischievous because it can mean several things: first, an annually defined administrative level (first grade, or fifth grade, for example); second, a judgmental indication of the relative skill or quality of a pupil's work when contrasted with the work of others;

third, a position on a scale of generally defined merit or worth; or fourth, a symbol of reaching a standard of some sort (e.g., to reach a certain level of accomplishment).

The term *nongraded* can therefore confuse some persons because unlike the examples just cited, it usually means that there exists a rejection, in the minds of teaching personnel and the parents with whom they connect, of procedures and vocabularies that seek to define the quality of each child's academic (and other) performance in the school as well as the child's status within the school community. While it is in fact appropriate for words, and even symbols, to be used that help to indicate both the level and the quality of a child's academic performance, it is not acceptable to approach this function in ways that seek to view the child primarily within a competitive context. By use of terms such as nongradedness in their interfaculty conversations and in their contacts with parents, if, and when, appropriate to the question being examined, teachers can develop or invent other vocabularies for use in discussing and even evaluating pupils and the progress they are making toward fulfilling their potential.

Nongradedness is both a mindset and an organizational pattern, and although the term is a bit awkward, it seeks to announce that the pupils within the educational environment are living and working under conditions that minimize their sense of competitiveness and that enable them to concentrate almost entirely upon activities that seem both manageable and challenging to them. A corollary consideration is that although each pupil is comfortably dealing with his or her own strengths and limitations, he or she is, within the same environment, able to connect intellectually (and socially, no doubt) with the full range of other pupils as opportunity is made available. Stated in operational terms, although each pupil's special and central responsibility is to make steady progress within his or her own focused academic agenda, each child is privileged to interact intellectually and personally with other pupils whose individual strengths and interests might at this moment be at a higher or lower level but who nevertheless can contribute understandings and interests that "enrich" the learning atmosphere or that invite the reexamination of ideas, skills, and attitudes.

It seems altogether reasonable to argue that deliberately heterogeneous multi-age grouping practices are by far more productive for pupil learning, and overall well-being, than are/were age-based or ability-based arrangements. For countless decades the validity of the latter arrangements has been unproven. Beginning with kindergarten, where at the outset some children are almost one year older (or younger) than their classmates, there is also an almost astonishing range within each pupil group of experiences, talents, and backgrounds. This reality continues to be present in the ensuing years when among other factors promotion and/or non-promotion policies cause the range of ages and experiences to become even greater. In fact, it is nearly impossible to assemble groups of children whose members are actually "homogeneous" in any relevant dimension of their daily school experience. Yet in nearly all schools almost every classroom group (e.g., for reading or mathematics instruction) is usually organized in terms of supposedly shared histories, talents, interests, and accomplishments.

On the other hand, the great majority of pupils, presented with an opportunity to associate academically with a larger number of other children, proved to be enthusiastic. They also welcomed the opportunity to connect with a number of teachers, each with his or her unique talents and interests, and especially to appreciate working alongside a larger, and therefore more versatile, group of fellow students. In conventional classroom situations, there are usually some strong pupils who tend to enjoy more teacher approbation and to become, almost habitually, the "leaders" in the group. In the same room, on the other hand, there are usually one or more kids with problems or histories of nonsuccess. One of the great discoveries during the early years of team teaching was that within the larger population of pupils, it became more possible for the nonsuccess kids to discover and connect with each other and at the same time it was easier to discover and utilize the one (or more!) teacher(s) who found excitement and pleasure in working with them.

The Goodlad/Anderson volume was reissued in 1987, and it is likely that this final version is available. One of my doctoral students at Harvard, who eventually became a close friend and partner, was Barbara Pavan. Dr. Pavan and I prepared and published (in 1993) a volume titled *Nongradedness: Helping It to Happen*. I suspect that now, in 2006, the book deserves recognition for the recency as well as the thoroughness of its material.

Before educators in the 21st century hasten to negative conclusions about the motivations and assumptions of teachers and other educational practitioners in the 19th century, and even during the early decades of the 20th century, it should be noted that the educational patterns and habits that grew in size and significance after 1848 were more or less accurately attuned to the prevailing mindset(s) of what might well have been the majority of adult citizens about children and what can or might be assumed about their potential, both academically and in dimensions of meritorious living. Even in the 21st century, by the way, it is possible to find at least some classrooms and even schools where these negative mindsets and correlated practices tend to exist and even, sad to say, to prevail. Much more probable, it seems possible to say, is that most teachers and the schools in which they work are well aware and very appreciative of the positive climate within which they are privileged to work. Even more wonderful, of course, would be that most pupils also function, cheerfully and productively, within a positive and supportive environment.

There were several reasons, all regrettable when viewed a century or more later, for the fixation that supported the pattern of classroom self-containment and the accompanying suspicion of the motives and the intellectual capabilities of children. As noted earlier, not only teachers but physicians, healthcare workers, and others entrusted with the well-being and development of future adults also had lower status many years ago than they have in today's (i.e., 21st century) world. However, of the groups mentioned, only school workers have remained at the financial mercy of their clients, probably because the financial support of excellent and currently up-to-date schooling (for all children, in every stratum of the society) would in many respects be significantly unaffordable from the taxpayers' viewpoint.

It seems important to note at this point that definitions of acceptable professional practice and the sufficiency of training of school workers have lagged very, very far behind the levels that obtain in comparable work settings. The enormous size and the universality of public education have complicated the problem of updating professional education. Even in the 21st century, it seems almost embarrassing to admit that there are no training programs for educators that are even a fraction as demanding and efficacious as those available to other categories of workers for whom the adjective "professional" seems appropriate. The situation is worsened by the calamitous shortage of appropriate candidates for teaching positions.

SUMMARY

In a world that children richly deserve and almost desperately need, having many connections with each other and many relationships with talented and caring adults can offer a much-to-be-desired atmosphere. Productive and stimulating connections with many "others" can make life far more stimulating, and therefore more motivating, for both adults and children than life in more conventional settings. It is greatly to be hoped that even small steps in the direction of these ideas can be very productive as well as rewarding. May each of these small steps encourage us to "think large" in the process.

The preceding paragraph may seem and probably is extreme in its implications for school practice. Schooling, even in the wealthiest and/or most enlightened communities and in most if not all highly reputed public as well as private schools, rarely reflects a sufficient and dedicated awareness of what might be labeled as the "musts" of excellent schooling. Alas, even in colleges and universities those "musts" are usually not pursued with passion and skill.

However, mentioning these flaws in the existing system is not intended to scold, and it is especially important for us not to abandon hope for significant progress and improvement. The goal should be for all of us to think more creatively about how to move from not-yet-close-enough to making-substantial-progress in a good direction.

Chapter Seven

Approaching Systems Thinking in Schools by Linking Quality and Sustainability

Moving from Theory to Practice

Anna Mårtensson and Kristen M. Snyder

Sustainability, as a concept and framework for living and work, has strengthened in recent decades fostering a mindset and way of living that stresses the importance of long-term thinking and planning to ensure that the decisions made today by individuals, businesses, and whole nations consider the needs and impact on society in the future (Lowe Steffen et al., 2019).

Two guideposts behind this evolution are the United Nations Agenda 2030 and the Sustainable Development Goals (SDGs), which concretize Agenda 2030 into 17 target areas (Sachs, 2015). The UN sustainability goals offer a powerful framework for addressing primary global challenges, such as generating economic growth, achieving social justice, exercising environmental stewardship, and strengthening governance. The global imperative to address sustainable development calls for organizations to reexamine their practices to meet complex societal challenges (Hawkins, 2018; Mårtensson et al., 2019).

New organizational systems need to meet customer needs, while being grounded and stable for building the kinds of healthy work environments that invite innovation and creativity to support sustainable development (Snyder & Snyder, 2021; Uhl-Bien & Arena, 2018). Current research in quality management includes sustainability as a key component of quality, expanding the notion of the customer to include society (Deleryd & Fundin, 2020). This perspective expands how we think about the interrelationship between sustainable organizational development and sustainable societal development.

The internal work systems, routines, and practices will necessarily need to integrate and link with sustainable societal development goals (Mårtensson et al., 2019; Ramanathan, 2021). Among the organizational actors, education has been singled out by UNESCO as essential to achieving sustainable development, articulating a new agenda to reorient education to help people develop knowledge skills, values, and behaviors needed for sustainable development (UNESCO, 2020).

The UN argues that obtaining a quality education is the foundation to improve people's lives and sustainable development (United Nations, 2017). Toward this end, educational policy in most countries now articulates the importance for schools to help children and youth develop knowledge and skills to respond to current and future challenges in society (Halinen, 2017; United Nations, 2017).

In the last several decades we have witnessed changes in curriculum development that stimulate learning about environmental issues, social justice, and the like. International tests, such as PISA, articulate the importance of measuring global citizenship and skills in cultural sensitivity (Organisation for Economic Co-operation and Development [OECD], 2001) as necessary indicators of quality in schools for a sustainable future. While these advancements are significant, they are not enough to help schools develop quality systems that address the pressing needs of a sustainable future.

As Snyder claims, "simply adding global competence, or other skills to the curriculum will fail to sustain a school's performance in modern times" (Snyder, 2019, p. 145). Leading sustainable development in schools requires a leadership mind-shift that includes a systems perspective that integrates structures, people, and processes with the sustainable development goals as guideposts (Snyder & Snyder, 2021).

Advancing schools toward sustainable development can be supported by bridging forces between quality management and sustainable development theory. Quality management, which is rooted in systems thinking and continuous improvement, can help organizations respond to changing conditions over time and keep organizations on the path to sustainability.

In this chapter, we illustrate how sustainable development, as both a concept and goal, can be integrated in a school's strategic management systems and operational programming to achieve sustainable quality development. Systems thinking and long-term thinking are two strategic concepts that are highlighted to help educational leaders develop schools that are adaptive and responsive to the changing needs of students and society.

In the first section of the chapter, quality management as an approach to organizational excellence is presented to set the stage for a systemic theoretical approach to leading. Within this framework, the concepts of systems theory and long-term thinking are presented as well. The second section of the chapter illustrates how quality management, systems thinking, and long-term thinking can be applied in a high-performing school to support the sustainable development goals.

QUALITY MANAGEMENT

Quality management today is an approach to organizational development that is designed around a systematic process that connects customer needs and organizational values and goals, with strategic planning, with the organization's culture and structures to continuously improve services and products for customers and stakeholders (Bergman & Klefsjö, 2020; Deming, 1986). Over the years, it has become a popular notion and philosophy for guiding work processes to meet the needs of customers.

Quality management is interpreted as *"management for quality"* by Klefsjö et al. (2008, p. 125). Bergman and Klefsjö (2020), address quality management through the "Cornerstone model," a model that includes six different components, defined as values by the authors. Together these six components represent an integrated whole, which when integrated, are more powerful than the individual components. Below are the six components of the Cornerstone model presented:

- *Focus on processes*, through repetitive work processes transform resources to results
- *Improve continuously*, continuously improve products, offers, and processes
- *Base decisions on fact*, informed decision making by collecting and analyzing information
- *Let everybody be committed*, by teaming and collaboration create meaningful, stimulating, and responsible tasks to benefit from all competencies
- *Focus on customers*, identify the customers and their needs and expectations, and finally fulfill them
- *Committed leadership*, engaged leadership which exemplifies a quality culture

The six components function interdependently as a system of functions that connect the strategic and operational levels in an organization. The concept of systems thinking is central for creating organizational cultures that are adaptive and responsive. A systems view of life creates the mindset that everyone is working together toward a common purpose (Capra & Luisi, 2016). A systems approach is a shift toward a multidisciplinary strategy for development, is relationship oriented, embraces mapping possibilities rather than evaluation systems, and measures success in quality, values, and process.

Long-term success with quality is dependent on managing the organization as one system to ensure alignment of needs, goals, structures, and organizational culture. Jonker (2000) adds that the long-term strategies and plans that are characteristics of quality management promote stability in the community, and at the same time deliver requested values to customers. Barnett et al. (2017) describes "long-term thinking" as a process in which actions and results are considered from both a short-term perspective and a long-term perspective, which are both future and immediate at the same time.

"Long-term planning" is the formulation of a strategy to meet the future. Pinedo (2004), adds that "Thinking" also includes the influence of the organization's vision and describes "Planning" as the movement from present to future. One of the big challenges for leaders today is shifting from a short-term, quick-fix mentality to long-term visioning and planning. Lowe Steffen et al. (2019) suggest this is needed if organizations of all kinds are to meet the SDGs.

Senge (2006) points out that there is an important relationship between commitments in a long term, like visions, and the individual core values among employees that influence decision making on a daily basis. If the gap between the vision and core values is too big, the organization will lose momentum and thereby become unsustainable. He reinforces the notion that all activities and decisions made today provide synergies that reach far beyond today's actions. To manage the complexity of synergies that will be an influence over a long term and also stretch over system boundaries requires skills in system thinking (Senge & Sterman, 1991).

Developing schools based on a systems view, in which long-term thinking and planning are applied, is based on the interdependence of strategic and operational levels. These two levels need to work together to achieve the desired goals, an organizational culture necessary for sustaining quality in complex times (Ingelsson & Mårtensson, 2014; Leithwood et al., 2020).

At the strategic level vision, policies, values, and principles are found, which serve as guideposts for the organization. These are translated into structures, processes, decision making, and actions at the operational level. Laszlo and Zhexembayeva (2011) also found an important interdependence between the strategic and operational levels for sustainable development. For example, organizations that integrated the values of sustainability and also translated them into operational practice created conditions important to reaching broader goals in sustainable development as outlined in Agenda 2030.

As part of the systems approach, Leithwood et al. (2020) describe the significant link between school leadership and staff involvement at the strategic level, reinforcing the interdependence between the strategic and operational levels. Further, they suggest there is an important connection between the organization's vision and what employees perceive is important. In a traditional school, teachers are often involved in decisions at the classroom level, yet removed from strategic planning. Leading schools from a systems perspective involves staff members in all levels of decision making.

Ingelsson and Mårtensson (2014) also found evidence of a lack of connection between the strategic and operational levels. In this study, the organization chose to focus on an overall continuous improvement system at the strategic level. However, the employees did not perceive they had sufficient insight or knowledge about the organization as a whole and were not heavily invested. For them, the system was not visible, and consequently, they did not find it to be important.

Other studies have demonstrated the importance for employees to have concrete methods and tools to complete tasks that are in line with the organization's strategic levels. This is often a missing element. Vandenbrande (2019) points out that quality methods and tools are available for all kinds of organizations, not just multinational organizations with extensive economic resources. The tools and methods are free to use. What matters is the vision and mission that guide the direction and goals of the organization (Vandenbrande 2019).

Case Study: Corbett Preparatory School of IDS

Corbett Preparatory School of IDS (CPS) in Tampa, Florida, is an independent school, with students from preschool through eighth grade, with stable leadership and teaching staff. This study was conducted in 2019 when Dr. Joyce Burick Swarzman was still leading the school, which she had done for over 25 years. The majority of the teaching staff has also been on campus for more than five years and many for over 10 years.

The school is known for its integrated curriculum that is designed around the International Baccalaureate (IB) program. The IB program is a well-established framework used in many schools throughout the world that is designed to integrate subjects with skills with social development to prepare for life in the globalized 21st century. The school is also a "lighthouse school" for the International School Connection, Inc. integrating the Global Learning Benchmarks (GLBs) into school life for many years (Sullivan, 2019).

The Global Learning Benchmarks support the OECD PISA Global Competence Framework to assist educators in increasing global competence in each child through classroom-based activities (Organisation for Economic Co-operation and Development [OECD], 2018). The IB program framework and GLBs are integrated into the school's systems to support global learning as a key feature of the school's academic and social environment.

The empirical data used in this chapter were collected during the autumn of 2019 prior to a shift in school leadership. Data were gathered through interviews, observations, notes taken during round tours, and document readings. The interviews were conducted with the (former) head of school, one associate head of school, two division leaders, two of the ISC developers of the Global Learning Benchmarks, one teacher, and the office manager.

Observations were carried out and documented in observation templates. Among the observations were one management meeting, one division meeting, and classroom teaching. Field notes were also written during tours of the school and included different activities. Selected documents were analyzed to increase the understanding of the school structures, programs, and purposes, and to obtain clarification of the school's work processes.

Guiding Principles for Learning, Teaching, and Organizing: A Systems Orientation

Corbett Preparatory School of IDS is grounded in a value-based organizational culture that recognizes teachers as the "most influential variable in the student learning process." The organizational culture and the supporting principles are compiled into a system that supports all activities throughout the school. This system, called M.O.R.E. (More Options for Results in Education), was developed over the decades by Joyce Swarzman.

In the book *It's All About Kids* by Cohen (2003), the school's founding model and principles for learning, teaching, and organizing are captured. The M.O.R.E. model is designed around seven research-based components that together make up the system of teaching and learning. The model represents a systemic view and foundational process to support teaching and learning.

The seven components have evolved through a commitment to continuous improvement and reflects educational best practices, brain-based research, common sense, and attention to uniting intellect with social, emotional, and body intelligence. The seven components include (1) child-centered vision, (2) appreciating the uniqueness of the learner, (3) motivational strategies to increase time on task, (4) creating dignity and respect, (5) teacher presence-making connections, (6) learning community, and (7) curriculum development.

During an interview with Joyce Swarzman in 2019, she described the school's 25-year development during her time as headmaster. The model she drew for us indicated that there are seven systems in place to support the vision and goals of the school, in which the M.O.R.E. model serves as the guiding foundation. The systems include (1) the four-pillars of well-being, (2) Gifted Education, (3) Cooperative Learning, (4) Global Learning Benchmarks, (5) Conceptual-Based Curriculum, (6) International Baccalaureate (IB), and (7) Cross-Curricular planning and multi-age grouping.

Each of these seven systems has a team of leaders who meet together regularly to plan and design the curriculum. All teachers in the school receive competence development in each of the systems to secure their capacity to participate in both implementation and continuous improvement to meet the needs of students. The system of seven components, including the M.O.R.E. model, match well with the quality management's Cornerstone model. For example, the customer focus is reflected in the multidimensionality of the brain-based learning environment designed to ensure that all students have the necessary conditions for excellence.

The Gobal Learning Benchmarks and IB standards provide guideposts for long-term thinking that connect curriculum development to the SDGs. Competence development and teaming support a culture of inclusion and participation that reinforces both engagement and commitment to the organization, its goals, vision, and customers. Multi-age grouping, gifted education, and the pillars of well-being support value-based competencies that are identified by international policy necessary to support SDGs, thus reflecting a long-term commitment to the future.

Teachers and students collectively shape learning goals that connect to the core principles and values associated with global sustainable development. Different pictures are hanging in the classrooms that illustrate the importance of weaving together character, care for the environment, creativity, and human development. Other pictures visualize a systems perspective for learning in which all subjects are integrated within an international framework that connects to SDGs and mindsets for a future society.

Each subject area is explored through a variety of projects, both community-based and individually based to reinforce the interconnectedness of people to a larger community of service. Within these approaches to teaching and learning is found a commitment to well-being, brain-based learning, and teaming. Accordingly, the school invests time, energy, and money in continuous staff development to help teachers stay on the cutting edge of learning opportunities. On the school's website, it is articulated that the school's policy and value-based commitment to staff development

> respects and recognizes the teacher as the key to the future.... We have focused on training specifically to support their valuable work in developing human potential for learning and living that will leave a legacy for which we can all be proud. (Corbett Preparatory School of IDS, 2022)

This investment in staff development has a direct correlation to the school's primary customer focus: the kids. It reflects a long-term investment in kids that is led by the actions of teachers today. The teaching and learning systems reflect a commitment to participation and shared leadership, informed decision making, clearly articulated work processes, and engaged leadership. The most important asset to the school is its people, with an "Olympic mentality," which translates to "a school as a community of learners that unites together to put children first, where everything speaks toward building confidence, character, creativity, and a caring heart for themselves and their students."

This value-based message is reinforced in the school's credo that hangs on the wall of the school auditorium in which whole-school meetings take place weekly. The heading indicates that the school is preparing children for life in the 21st century, in which human characteristics are fostered to support the principles of a democratic society, which is part of their sustainable development platform. The "weapons" are language skills and behaviors that foster peace and caring for self and others.

Interlinking Quality Management and Sustainability in Practice

Let us now consider how Corbett Preparatory School illustrates the six components of the Cornerstone model in practice. The Cornerstone model (Bergman & Klefsjö, 2020), like all quality management models, reflects a systems perspective for leading and sustaining continuous quality improvement. The components in the model are (1) focus on processes, (2) improve continuously, (3) base decisions on fact, (4) let everybody be committed, (5) focus on customers, and (6) committed leadership.

When using the Cornerstone model as a framework to identify practice within CPS, multiple dimensions reinforce the notion that sustaining quality in organizations is based on the interdependence of functions and processes. For example, in *focus on the process*, several characteristics within the organization's culture were identified among the school leaders, the division leaders, teachers, and the supporting functions. Among them are the regularity of meetings, structure for meetings, the regular use of reflection and dialogue, and application of tools such as the "five whys" and "fist of five" for voting.

To secure the flow of communication throughout the organizations, meetings were scheduled throughout the week during which information was shared at the different levels. This scheduling model, which could be likened to the domino effect, ensured that the entire staff was both informed, and also given ample space in which to dialogue in smaller groups about the information. This served as an architectural aspect of the school's organization that was used to foster deep learning and engagement.

Under the second cornerstone, *improve continuously*, the school and division leaders and teachers illustrated various ways in which continuous improvement serves as a guidepost for the school. As one leader shared, "We constantly are looking at what works and what needs to be better." A common practice in meetings was to ask the *five whys* when exploring an issue to get at the root cause of a scenario. The M.O.R.E. model evolved over time, and over years, as a response to the need for continuous improvement. Teachers reported a culture of experimentation in the classroom encouraging students to learn from and with one another.

The use of research, information, analysis, and dialogue, was prevalent in the descriptions at all levels regarding the third cornerstone, *basing decisions on fact*. This was supported by both process and structure for meetings. The school leaders and division leaders reported the importance of regular meetings, and reflections on progress toward goals as central to their daily work. It was evident that the information discussed reflected current practices as it related to the values of the school and a focus on the customer.

We often heard echoes of questions from teachers, such as "How have we done it before and how are we doing it now?" as a reflective practice to learn from history. The work structure and processes for a meeting, dialogue, and reflection were grounded in strong values that reflected a commitment to helping each child develop themselves as strong global citizens. The history of the M.O.R.E. model illustrates a journey that leaves nothing to chance, for each part of the school's continuous improvement journey is rooted in research.

There was evidence of a strong sense of commitment, engagement, and participation among all staff and leaders as part of the cornerstone, *let everybody be committed* and *committed to leadership*. For example, the staff was provided with competence development regularly to reinforce their capacity for commitment and leadership. As well, meeting agendas were co-created and based on the needs of kids as identified by the teaching staff and division leaders.

As one teacher shared, "We build teams based on our interest when working with global competence." And another teacher shared, "There is a really strong need for passion and commitment to what we are doing to make it all work." At the classroom level, students participate and shape their classroom goals and values. Evidence of this was observed in each room, with value-based words lining the walls to visualize the kind of engaged leadership that permeates the school's culture.

The headmaster and associate headmaster spend time walking through the school, meeting and greeting students, parents, and teachers, and listening to their perspectives about what makes the school great. This illustrates the engagement of leaders in the daily activities of the school. In quality management terms, we can say that the school's leaders have created a culture of "Gemba Walking" in which they regularly observe, ask questions, engage in dialogue, solve problems, and even jump into the classroom at times as an extra hand.

Students at the school are given opportunities to develop their leadership skills in programs such as "Leader Mentors" and "Headmaster of School for a Day," reflecting the school's value and commitment to participation and engagement at all levels from the principal to the student. As part of the multi-age focus, leader mentors were developed in which second-year students come to school early to learn about leadership and mentoring and are then paired with first-year students.

The "Headmaster of the Day" program is offered to kids of all ages who want to develop their leadership skills and want the opportunity to follow the school's leader for a day. In preparation, the students are given training in leadership, are asked to run meetings, and participate in school leadership under the mentorship of the school's head. Such programs illustrate the strong customer focus and long-term thinking that is designed to help kids develop a variety of skills for success in life.

The final cornerstone, *customer focus*, permeates the language and behaviors of staff and leaders in the school. This is seen in the motto of the school, "It's All About the Kids" and the core of the M.O.R.E. model with a focus on "creating a brain-friendly environment to accelerate the learning process." The students, seen as customers, are invited to shape life in their classroom, cowrite the goals and values for their learning environment, and participate in shaping their learning teams. The curriculum is designed around SDGs and a set of skill-based competencies for contributing to and succeeding in a democratic global community.

Curriculum planning and the classroom environments are designed with variety in mind to ensure that each student's unique needs are met. According to one division leader, they see themselves "as helping children to acquire a language in their role as global citizens. Another teacher and division leader shared that

> the work with global learning with the students is seen as building skills. It mirrors beautifully with your creative thinking and your outside of the box, collaboration and cooperation with other people. The hope is that the skills students are trained in affect how they see the world. Global learning is a lifelong skill

that they will take seriously and understand a little more about how it can impact their lives. (Division leader at Corbett Prep., 2019)

A focus on the customer is visible throughout the school, from the walkways lined with signs of positive thinking and positive phrasing to the walls in the classroom lined with values and character traits for a sustainable future. The strong visual presence reinforcing such values illustrates one of the ways in which the school practices long-term thinking. For kids to be successful in contributing to a sustainable democratic society they need to be the best they can be and possess skills and competencies to contribute to sustaining the future.

We found evidence of this at both the strategic and operational levels, which reinforced the presence of a systems orientation in the school. For example in the elementary school, at the teaching level, the systems for cooperative learning and conceptual-based cross-curriculum (strategic level) provided the structural framework within which lesson plans (operational level) related to how the Global Learning Benchmarks and SDGs (strategic level) were designed. One of the teachers described how they plan in teaching teams based on an integrated curriculum in which the Global Learning Benchmarks are central:

> The primary year's program has the opportunity to create a planner and so they give us certain criteria about global benchmarks ... standards they have for global benchmarks and we made them part of our planner. So, when a teacher sits down to plan and consider what standards and concepts they are addressing. They are also looking at what GLBs they will be addressing. (Interview of teacher at Corbett Prep., 2019)

The integrated curriculum design (strategic level) for the school and team teaching (strategic and operational levels) enhances possibilities for the staff to continuously reinforce the behaviors and values (strategic and operational levels) for sustainable development. It provides a structure through teaming, as well as a systems orientation to planning. There are core elements related to value-based development that are integrated into learning modules. For example, values of respect and listening are included under the broader heading of democracy and citizenship development.

CONCLUSIONS

This case study illustrates how a high-performing school functions with a foundation in values that support quality management, long-term thinking, and systems thinking. Evidence from Corbett Preparatory School provides insights into the importance of a systems perspective and long-term thinking for creating conditions necessary for schools to become sustainable.

Clearly defined functions and processes that are grounded in the values and goals of the organization create conditions for educators to continuously meet the needs of their students. The school system also reinforces the quality management principles of commitment, engagement, and skill-based training to provide employees with the knowledge and skills to deliver a cutting-edge service.

At the school, the customer was clearly defined and central in all dialogues and decisions. Long-term thinking was found to be a grounding mechanism used in decision making, as well as an approach to continuous improvement. Its presence and function in the school were both visible in the dialogues among staff and the curriculum planning based on the IB and GLB. Long-term thinking was also found to be an espoused value deeply interwoven into the philosophical fabric of the school's culture.

This study also contributes with greater insights into understanding organizations through the lens of the *emergence paradigm* in which teaming, networking, collaboration, and the principle of self-organization are central to achieving quality. This case also illustrates how organizations can develop integrated systems that connect the principles and practices of quality management to the principles, practices, and goals of sustainability. In so doing, sustainable development can be seen as both an end goal as well as a value-based approach to living, learning, and organizing.

Current research in the area of quality management and sustainability has demonstrated the need to improve the linkages between practice and theory. While there is a clear connection between values espoused in quality management and sustainable development, the two are often kept separate at the organizational level. As such, there is a recognized need for understanding how organizational leaders can integrate the practices of quality management with the goals of sustainability such that they act together as a system to foster continuous organizational improvement.

Lessons learned from Corbett Preparatory School of IDS suggest that committed leaders and dedicated employees are needed to constantly develop the business. There is also a need for access to reliable information that is connected to a clearly articulated mission with a strong customer focus. In this particular school, customer focus was found to be a significant, if not the most significant factor in the organization's application of long-term thinking through which they translated theory and policy into practice at all levels of the organization.

CALL TO ACTION

Educators, the choice is yours: developing sustainable schooling is within reach when linking quality management and long-term thinking together in a system of interdependent work functions. Children and youth are the next generations, and it is on your shoulders to move past the political winds that change on a dime and create quality environments in schools that meet the needs of a sustainable future.

Systems are needed in schools that build from knowledge to create space for innovation and engagement for all. The value of continuous improvement, along with participatory practice and shared principles, becomes the structure needed that sends forth youth with their own backpacks filled with knowledge, skills, and confidence to lead a future that is sustainable and ever evolving.

REFERENCES

Barnett, T., Bowes, M. J., White, J., & Zaib, A. (2017). Long-term thinking in organizations. *SAGE Publications, 21*(2), 109–128.

Bergman, B., & Klefsjö, B. (2020). *Kvalitet från behov till användning.* Studentlitteratur AB, Lund (in Swedish).

Capra, F., & Luisi, P. L. (2016). *The systems view of life: A unifying vision.* Cambridge University Press.

Cohen, D. (2003). *It's all about kids: Every child deserves a "Teacher of the Year."* Bee Happy Publishing.

Corbett Preparatory School of IDS. (2022, March). https://www.corbettprep.com/

Deleryd, M., & Fundin, A. (2020). Towards societal satisfaction in a fifth generation of quality—The sustainability model. *Total Quality and Business Excellence.*

Deming, E. W. (1986). *Out of the crisis.* MIT, Center for Advanced Educational Services.

Halinen, I. (2017). *The conceptualization of competencies related to sustainable development and sustainable lifestyles.* UNESCO: International Bureau of education series, current and critical issues in curriculum, learning and assessment, 8.

Hawkins, M. J. (2018). Developing a perspective on schools as complex, evolving loosely linking systems. *Educational Management Administration & Leadership, 46*(5), 729–748.

Ingelsson, P., & Mårtensson, A. (2014). Measuring importance and practices of lean values. *The TQM Journal, 26*(5), 463–474.

Jonker, J. (2000). Organizations as responsible contributors to society: Linking quality, sustainability and accountability. *Total Quality Management, 11*(4–6), 741–746.

Klefsjö, B., Bergquist, B., & Garvare, R. (2008). Quality management and business excellence, customers and stakeholders. Do we agree on what we are talking about, and does it matter? *The TQM Journal, 20*(2), 120–129.

Laszlo, C., & Zhexembayeva, N. (2011). *Embedded sustainability—The next big competitive advantage*. Stanford University Press.

Leithwood, K., Harris, A., & Hopkins, D. (2020). Seven strong leadership claims about successful school leadership revisited. *School Leadership & Management, 40*(1), 5–22.

Lowe Steffen, S., Rezmovitz, J., Trevenna, S., & Rappaport, S. (2019). *Evolving leadership for collective wellbeing*. Emerald Publishing Limited.

Mårtensson, A., Snyder, K., & Ingelsson, P. (2019). Interlinking lean and sustainability: How ready are leaders? *The TQM Journal, 31*(2), 136–149.

Organisation for Economic Co-operation and Development [OECD]. (2001). *Education at a glance. OECD Indicators 2001*. OECD/Centre for Educational Research and Innovation.

Organisation for Economic Co-operation and Development [OECD]. (2018). *PISA 2018 global competence*. Retrieved from http://www.oecd.org/pisa/pisa-2018-global-competence.htm

Pinedo, V. (2004). *Tsunami: Building organizations capable of prospering in tidal waves.* iUniverse.

Ramanathan, N. (2021). Quality-based management for future-ready corporations serving society and planet. *Total Quality Management & Business Excellence, 32*(5–6), 541–557.

Sachs, J. (2015). *The age of sustainable development*. Colombia University Press.

Senge, P. (2006). *The fifth discipline: The art and practice of the learning organization*. Currency and Doubleday.

Senge, P., & Sterman, J. (1991). Systems thinking and organizational learning: Acting locally and thinking globally in the organization of the future. *European Journal of Operational Research, 59*, 137–150.

Snyder, K. J. (2019). Preparing globally competent students: The K–12 schooling challenge. Advances in Global Education and Research. *GLOCER 19: Advances in Global Education and Research, 3*, 126–135.

Snyder, K. J., & Snyder, K. M. (2021). Building sustainable systems for schooling in turbulent times: Big ideas from the sciences. In. Jeffrey Glanz (Ed.), *Crisis and pandemic leadership: Implications for meeting the needs of students, teachers, and parents*. Rowman & Littlefield Publishers.

Sullivan, E. (2019). Global Learning Benchmark Integration Project at Corbett Preparatory School. *GLOCER 19: Advances in Global Education and Research, 3*, 126–135.

Uhl-Bien, M., & Arena, M. (2018). Leadership for organizational adaptability: A theoretical synthesis and integrative framework. *The Leadership Quarterly, 29*, 89–104.

United Nations. (2017). "Resolution adopted by the General Assembly on 20 December 2017," in G. Assembly (Ed.), 72/222, 2018, p. 1. https://undocs.org/en/A/RES/72/222

United Nations Educational, Scientific and Cultural Organization [UNESCO]. (2020). *Education for sustainable development: A roadmap.* https://unesdoc.unesco.org/ark:/48223/pf0000374802.locale=en

Vandenbrande, W. W. (2019). Quality for a sustainable future. *Total Quality Management & Business Excellence, 32*(5–6), 467–475.

Chapter Eight

Appreciative School Systems
A Path to School Success
John Mann

External forces are attacking the very fiber of education while politicians search for, among other things, ways to dictate curriculum and instruction strategies. Assessment is still being used to rank and sort teachers and schools rather than serving as a critical diagnostic tool to support continuous improvement. The pandemic has created unparalleled stress levels on a system that was already very fragile. Exhausted and exasperated, teachers are leaving at unprecedented rates (Walker, 2022).

At the same time, since 2006, many universities have produced over 40% fewer graduates with degrees in education (Goldberg, 2021). Fewer people consider leadership positions, and many leaders feel their hands are tied without a positive way out. If all we ever do is focus on the problems, we will only see things that need to be fixed and lose sight of our strengths and possibilities for growth.

Deficit thinking has been hardwired into most educational systems through data analysis, problem solving, change strategies, personnel, students, and dealing with issues of the day. Using an appreciative lens while dealing with problematic areas is an antidote to deficit thinking. Albert Einstein stated, "No problem can be solved from the same level of consciousness that created it" (James, n.d., number 53). Viewing an issue from a nondeficit lens by focusing on what is possible and using appreciative strategies are steps toward a more positive future. Using the strengths of individuals and organizations further supports a distinct and productive journey.

Appreciative Inquiry (AI) and the complementary work of Martin Seligman in Positive Psychology become that antidote. The emphasis on treating people well while focusing on personal and organizational strengths, as an alternative to a deficit-oriented way of analyzing data, opened up new doors of possibility (Barrett & Fry, 2005). It is exciting to focus on the power of gratitude and helping people while creating an organization that appreciates by leveraging strengths and building on the successes of its work. AI is changing the world when positive change is desperately needed, one collaborative strength-based step at a time.

The simple phrase "doing well by doing good" is often attributed to Benjamin Franklin and thought to be for businesses as Appreciative Inquiry was designed to be. With that in mind, Burrello et al. (2016) developed a framework around the mindset of Appreciative Inquiry for education organizations, which is called Appreciative Organizing in Education (AOE).

AOE supports leaders and organizations to create whole system coherence, which focuses on strengths, transcendent core purpose and values, generative communication, capacity building, and developing internal accountability. The goal of everything working together to benefit the whole system is ambitious, yet essential for creating successful and sustainable schools. Many public schools are successful, and even greater success is possible by using an appreciative systems approach.

This chapter explores how educators can develop the school as a whole system while creating sustainable paths for major categories of subsystems. They can be as small as the bus procedures or as big as the master schedule. Applying an appreciative approach to each subsystem enhances the overall system. We know that creating *a systems thinking* framework for programs and services, decision making and planning, building capacity, and collaborative culture while using a consistent data reflection cycle can be a path to success (Snyder et al., 2021).

Part 1 discusses the influential foundation Appreciative Inquiry provides for Appreciative Organizing in Education. It highlights the AOE framework and its critical aspects necessary in creating Whole System Coherence. Part 2 focuses on a research study of successful, appreciative leaders, their strategies, and their implications for future action. Part 3 offers a summary and a call to action, which focuses on why appreciative systems can create a successful and sustainable organization.

PART 1: APPRECIATIVE INQUIRY LEADS TO APPRECIATIVE ORGANIZING IN EDUCATION

Appreciative Inquiry (AI) is about creating systems that are working at their best. AOE would not be possible without the influence and work of David Cooperrider and his efforts in developing AI, which is an expression of collaboration, positive core, generativity, positivity, and strengths (Cooperrider & Whitney, 2005). The authors' state,

Appreciative Inquiry is about the co-evolutionary search for the best in people, their organizations, and the relevant world around them. In its broadest focus, it involves systematic discovery of what gives life to a living system when it is most alive, most effective, and most constructively capable in economic, ecological, and human terms. (Cooperrider & Whitney, 2005, p. 3)

In an interview with David Cooperrider, Peter Drucker stated, "The task of leadership is to create an alignment of strengths . . . making a system's weakness irrelevant" (Cooperrider & Whitney, 2005, p. 2). This idea gets to the heart of AI.

The five Appreciative Inquiry Principles are helpful in addressing the ever-increasing negative flow of the world today, which are critical to the development of AOE and its goal of creating appreciative and prosperous systems. Cooperrider and Whitney (2005) list them as the Constructionist Principle, Principle of Simultaneity, Poetic Principle, Anticipatory Principle, and Positive Principle. These five principles become critical and foundational as we think about developing a school as a system that focuses on strengths.

The Appreciative 4-D Cycle, which is synonymous with AI, can inspire the practical work of the day as well as provide the principles for the summit process. According to Cooperrider and Whitney (2011), an Appreciative Inquiry Summit is a way to bring a diverse group of stakeholders together to discover, design, and implement improvement strategies that are based on an organization's strengths. It can occur over one day or three to four days. A summit happens using the four Ds of Appreciative Inquiry (Cooperrider & Whitney, 2005):

- Discovery: Mobilizing the whole system by engaging all stakeholders in the articulation of strengths and best practices. Identifying "the best of what has been and what is."
- Dream: Creating a clear, results-oriented vision in relation to discovered potential and in relation to questions of higher purpose, such as "What is the world calling us to become?"
- Design: Creating possibility propositions of the ideal organization, articulating an organization design that people feel is capable of drawing upon and magnifying the positive core to realize the newly expressed dream.
- Destiny: Strengthening the affirmative capability of the whole system, enabling it to build hope and sustain momentum for ongoing positive change and high performance. (p. 16)

The AI Principles and Appreciative 4-D Cycle philosophy encourage us to seek new positive strength-based and appreciative ways of working as collaborative leaders. Leaders provide direction and, at times, build management systems to support the organization's day-to-day procedures and protocols, which are part of every subsystem. In that way, appreciative thinking can be the basis for everything we do. The work of appreciative leadership and appreciative organizing further demonstrates AI's influence on our actions (Whitney et al., 2010).

Cooperrider and Whitney (2005) remind us that organizations are primarily positive oriented, and it is up to us to recognize and focus on their strengths. We are trying to coordinate our efforts to be a part of the same positive wave with that in mind. This occurs when everyone is in the same boat rowing in the same direction in a synchronized effort. It is the only way that our major systems and subsystems can flourish.

The Appreciative Organizing in Education framework designed by Leonard Burrello, Linda Beitz, and John Mann (Figure 8.1) has six spheres and

Figure 8.1. Appreciative Organizing in Public Education: A Framework for Learning, Working, and Living Well Together. *Leonard C. Burrello, Linda M. Beitz, and John L. Mann, 2016.*

four guiding principles (Burrello et al., 2016). The purpose is to inspire educational leaders to develop appreciative strategies, philosophies, and structures to develop educational systems and ultimately obtain Whole System Coherence (WSC).

AOE illuminates a positive strengths-based approach to developing a school as a system that relies on relational leaders creating and using transcendent purposes and core values in their school communities. The system relies on a generative process dealing with external forces by focusing on and maximizing internal strengths to achieve whole system coherence.

The six spheres include Transcendent Core Purpose and Values; Positive Strengths; Relational Leadership; Generative Learning and Capacity Building; Internal and External Accountability; and Whole System Coherence. In AOE, the first five spheres are foundational and supportive of all the complex and simple subsystems that make up the day-to-day functions of a school. The key is that subsystems interact, interrelate, and collaborate to create WSC, supporting the achievement of goals. Whole System Coherence in a school is possible only when there is an understanding of all parts that make up the entire system.

The characteristics of being hopeful, fulfilled, connected, and resilient are the four guiding principles. As influenced by the guiding principles, each of the first five spheres is critical in developing the foundation for school success by creating major systems and subsystems. The major systems could be Safety and Security, Academics, and Human Resources. These three major systems have numerous subsystems critical to school success and can be as unique as the school's curriculum design to the bus dismissal procedures.

Under the major subsystem of Human Resources, a critical part is understanding the importance and power of human networks. There are individuals, small human network clusters, and major network clusters in every school. Each aspect of these ever-important networks is critical and linked with varying levels of influence and strength, dictating an organization's overall productivity and ultimate success.

We begin where we want to end with Whole System Coherence (WSC). To get to this complex destination, it is essential to align a culture where all things work together and are appreciated for their strengths and contributions. If we do not value the custodians' efforts and help them understand their importance to the school's overall success, why would they care or feel a part of the school community? Merriam-Webster (Merriam-Webster.com, n.d.) describes coherence or the properties of being coherent as containing the elements of consistency, understandability, cohesion, and coordination.

In the world of physics, we think of the property of a set of waves where everything is moving in the same way and direction, whether uniformly spread out or not (Norton, 2022). Our quest for WSC may be a career-long endeavor where leaders accept they are part of the living system. They acknowledge our influential supporting role and have a clear third-party vision of what is necessary to thrive in a successful living system.

Some have believed that managing the subsystems is all that is needed, but it is far from true. After knowing what to coordinate, determining how to interconnect all major systems and subsystems is essential for a successful living system. Knowledge of the foundational spheres of AOE, which are unpacked below, is critical to success.

Transcendent Core Purpose and Values

"Your beliefs become your thoughts, Your thoughts become your words, Your words become your actions, Your actions become your habits, Your habits become your values, Your values become your destiny" — Gandhi (Schindler, 2018). This critical area is essential for aligning major systems and subsystems to develop Whole System Coherence.

One of the first things that occurs is establishing a clear core purpose and values. Simon Sinek states that you must have an inspired, optimistic, and overarching "why" for what you hope to accomplish and become (Sinek, 2009). To articulate the real reason you are willing to get up and go to school should be the purpose of your work. Establishing the purpose collaboratively with the staff is important.

We begin with the core purpose but quickly have to establish the core values for the organization, which become the guide in support of the core purpose for all of the work and decisions in creating a preferred future. "Many visionary companies only have three to five core values or essential tenets for who they are" (Collins & Porras, 1996, p. 67). When working with constituents to create core values, ask if the idea will still be important in ten years. If the answer is yes, then you are on the right track.

As successful ethical leaders, it is essential to understand the intersection of our personal and professional values. A strong focus on values, whether it be three or ten, will help deal with the everyday pressures of leading an organization and dealing with consistent external forces.

Positive Strengths

We know from the research that the most effective leaders know their strengths and have learned that working from strengths increases engagement, happiness, and improved performance at work (Rath & Conchie, 2008). The use of positive strengths is a simple area to understand and difficult to develop and use at a deep level. The first step is to understand strengths. This can be achieved by participating in an individual strength survey; two of the most prominent are Clifton's Strengths-Finder 2.0 and Seligman's Values in Action Character Strengths (Niemiec, 2013).

Next is to get to know the staff's strengths and those of the teams, departments, and the school. After identifying the strengths, the hard part is determining how to highlight and use those strengths to benefit all. From their strengths, people will maximize the possibility of success and satisfaction. It can be used as the first step with data and strategies that might be implemented. Knowing how to use the strengths of all major systems and subsystems to create whole system coherence is key to organizational success.

Relational Leadership

We take the power of relationships in developing an organization for granted. The ever-important connections between people within a system can spell success or failure. "A relational leader instills hope in coworkers and employees, and is grateful for the work they do, and is always kind and fair in the ways they are treated" (Mann et al., 2018, p. 35). Networks within the system will seek direction and align themselves with influential forces. If we do not provide or support a positive influence, harmful or toxic energy will likely fill the vacuum.

A personal and powerful conviction about the importance of relationships will produce positive connections. Focusing on the seven Appreciative Organizing relational dispositions—caring, respectful, trustworthy, passionate, hopeful, grateful, and kind—will help fill the vacuum with positivity. Appreciation of the people in a school and the development of trust precede the heavy lifting necessary to succeed in school improvement and the development of whole system coherence.

Generative Learning and Capacity Building

We are always better together, and our positive questions make all the difference. Using questions to explore what is possible can assist people to think appreciatively. Consider positively reframing communications using more generative language. Developing others by investing in their lives should always be a point of focus. Using a generative focus and consistent strength-based development of capacity supports the development of the system.

Internal and External Accountability

Internal accountability is the answer to dealing with oppressive external forces. External accountability is necessary, and some of it is positive and pushes us to grow. Some of it is created by outside agencies for reasons practitioners might not believe helpful. The goal is not to be dominated by external forces but rather to have the courage to use core purpose and values to guide the work of the school. Internal accountability is key to how successful systems operate in the face of external forces.

PART 2: A STUDY OF SUCCESSFUL APPRECIATIVE LEADERS

Looking at what is possible and working toward a preferred future creates hope and a greater possibility of success. Nine leaders were interviewed who subscribed to an appreciative leadership approach to their work. Their insights helped inform a deeper understanding of the journey of AOE and the goal of reaching Whole System Coherence. The group consisted of elementary, middle, and high school principals, school district and college administrators, plus a person from private industry.

All participants are considered successful leaders because of achievement measures obtained within schools or their ability to build thriving organizations. Seven interviewees also were doctoral students or recent graduates, and the other two had already completed educational specialist degrees. Their insight will be shared and studied as we consider what has been gleaned in our goal to develop Whole System Coherence.

Through the interviews, an emphasis was placed on having coordinated subsystems that make the overall system intentional. In AOE, subsystems must be deliberate and adaptive to sustain positive growth and development. Subsystems were also described as a giant puzzle that flows together to be successful and viewed holistically with a clear understanding of where one hopes to end up. When one can see the positive future of the organization, then one can backward map the year through expectations of what will occur with each subsystem.

The interviewees identified four major themes: strengths; vision, purpose, and core values; relationships; and generative communication. These themes were frequent and significant areas and are identified as Themes 1–4. Two minor themes, *capacity building* and *internal accountability*, also emerged and are listed as Themes 5 and 6. The interviewees clearly emphasized essential aspects of accountability that generate a successful and appreciative organization. Each major and minor theme will be examined and considered for how it contributes to whole system coherence.

Theme 1: Strengths

Identifying and using strengths was the number one area mentioned in the interviews. Every person mentioned strengths as extremely important in developing whole system coherence, and most people emphasized it more than once.

The interview group used strengths to develop and support their systems in the following ways: build on and connect strengths; keep recentering by going back to strengths; understand the leader's strengths; know and use the strengths of the leadership team; know the strengths of all the teachers; commit to using strengths in every policy, procedure, and system in the school; acknowledge that the staff is the strength of our school; use strengths to problem solve, develop teams, coach, mentor, develop staff, and make academic plans for students; and help staff to be more productive and happier by working from their strengths.

Interviewees found they were more productive and successful by using strengths to improve individual performance as well as all areas of the school. Strengths might be a natural addition to the core values based on the research. Listed are the implications for the theme, strengths, and actions suggested by the research group. First, get to know the strengths of the staff and school. Take an honest inventory of the school's strengths and interview staff to discover their thoughts on the subject. Use either StrengthsFinder 2.0 or VIA Character Strengths to learn the individuals' strengths (Niemiec, 2013).

The principal sets an example for the rest of the school and commits to the process. Start with the leadership team or a volunteer department or team. Develop a plan with a steering committee on how to use the information to enhance the success and productivity of individuals and the school. Come up with a long-term goal of how to develop a strengths-led school and what that means.

One powerful systems-based strategy is to start converting policies, procedures, and subsystems from a deficit or neutral focus to a strengths focus. The use of strengths is the number one area the research group indicated there has to be concentrated action to assist the school to be as successful as possible and move to Whole System Coherence.

Theme 2: Vision, Purpose, and Core Values

During their interviews, the second most discussed theme that each expert practitioner mentioned was the importance of a positive vision, core values, or purpose as critical to their own success and the organization's success. The interview group used vision, core purpose, and values to develop and support their systems in the following ways: collaboratively develop the school's vision, core purpose, and values; success comes from applying core values to every work situation; and write the core values in a simple and understandable form.

Other ways the interview group used vision, core purpose, and values to develop and support their systems were: communicate the vision, core purpose, and values clearly and often; gain a clear picture (vision) of the organization and then backward map everything from there; know every major system and subsystem and that they work together in accordance with the core purpose and values; use core purpose and values in every decision made, and a successful and positive culture starts with positive core values.

Even with strengths being the number one theme, all interviewees stated that a successful systems approach to leadership could not be reached without vision, purpose, and core values. Listed are the implications for the theme Vision, Purpose, and Core Values, and the actions suggested by the research group.

First, make sure the vision or core purpose is optimistic and visionary. It highlights who one is or who one wants to be. The core values are concise and timeless. They hold moral and ethical meaning for how we make decisions and live together to create a school of excellence. The vision, purpose, and core values are known by everyone and communicated consistently. They are not just highlighted at the beginning of the year or when there is a formal presentation about the school. The journey toward a positive culture starts by placing the core values into action. Vision, purpose, and core values are vital to establishing a positive living system.

Theme 3: Relationships

The third theme taken from the interviews is the power and importance of relationships. Schools are unlikely to succeed and develop successful systems if they ignore the importance of human interaction and connections.

The interview group used relationships and relational leadership to develop and support their systems in the following ways: purposefully develop relationships consistently and intentionally; be visible and available; use an Appreciative Inquiry Summit as a tool to build trust and respect; make a goal of knowing each staff member personally; model positivity and caring by reaching out to others; establish ways for everyone to have input into the system; treat people the way they want to be treated (Platinum Rule; Hall, 2017); and be sincere in all communications.

When considering the subsystems of a school, a majority of the interviewees focused on people. Each one stated that developing whole system coherence is possible with a clear dedication to the development and sustainability of positive relationships. Listed are the implications for the Relationships themes and actions suggested by the research group.

First, no one can lead a school from the office. Get out every day for large parts of the day. Please sincerely communicate with the staff while getting to know them personally. Try to go beyond the Golden Rule to the Platinum Rule by treating people the way they want to be treated. Learn more about the importance and power of an Appreciative Inquiry Summit and use those ideas to enhance the school and its systems. A living system cannot reach whole system coherence without focusing on and understanding the power and potential of positive relationships.

Theme 4: Generative Communication/Positivity

Generative communication and positivity seem to go hand in hand. Generative communication was highlighted in every one of the experts' answers. The addition of positivity, while moving away from deficit thinking to what is possible, created a vital area. The interview group used generative communication and positivity to develop and support their systems in the following ways: use positive strength-based or appreciative questions to start every meeting, coaching, and mentoring session; focus on how one communicates by being positive and strengths forward; and increase the positive tone in written as well as verbal communication.

Other ways the interview group used generative communication and positivity to develop and support their systems were to look for positives and strengths of data and situations instead of focusing on weaknesses and deficits; develop a bank of appreciative questions to refer to for conversations, meetings, and coaching; be open and honest in all communication; remember, positive energy propels; smile a lot; be intentional and authentic in the positive actions taken as a leader; and let the school family know they are loved.

Interviewees commented that the theme Generative Communication and Positivity includes the following implications and actions. First, take every opportunity throughout the day, whether in general conversations, meetings, coaching, or mentoring sessions, to highlight strengths and create a clear, purposeful, and positive-focused culture. Be intentional. Always consider tone and actions in all verbal, written, and nonverbal gestures by consistently working to support people positively.

Prepare for meetings and conversations by creating a list of appreciative questions to use in meetings and discussions and practice ahead of time. Positivity propels kindness to others even in difficult situations.

Be authentic. Delivering bad news is never easy; however, showing respect is always appropriate no matter the case. The expert group opined on the importance and power of letting the school community know that they are appreciated through words or deeds. There was a universal feeling from interviewees that whole system coherence could not be reached without generative communication.

Theme 5: Internal Accountability

The area of internal accountability was highlighted primarily by the experts around the alignment of subsystems and major systems of the organization. The interview group used internal accountability, especially aligning subsystems to develop and support their systems in the following ways: core purpose and values should be considered in developing new policies, procedures, protocols, and forms; review policies, procedures, protocols, and forms and align them with an appreciative focus; and know all the school's major systems and subsystems.

Other ways the interview group used internal accountability was to check on all subsystems to make sure they are functioning correctly; have open, clear, and transparent communication throughout the organization's systems; and enhance and increase the integration, interconnectivity, and interdependence of significant areas and subsystems.

This area was viewed as important in developing a living and whole system. Each point was critical, but this area, though necessary, was not acknowledged by everyone. Listed are the implications for the theme Internal Accountability and actions suggested by the research group. First, focus on knowing the vision, purpose, and core values so that they can guide how one responds to outside pressures, which may or may not create an advantage for the school.

Identify and become knowledgeable of all the major systems and subsystems of the school. Then use the same purpose and values to enhance the integration and interdependence of all parts of the overall system. Have a vision of what one wants to accomplish and align the policies, procedures, protocols, and forms, which will allow an appreciative leadership focus to be a part of how the school and its systems work.

Theme 6: Capacity Building

The last minor theme, capacity building, was highlighted several times but did not approach the frequency of the themes discussed above. The interview group used capacity building to develop and support their systems in the following ways: provide professional development based on individual strengths; develop as many leaders as possible; work on mindset; focus on as much appreciative coaching and mentoring as possible; and be purposeful with the development of culture.

Listed are the implications for the theme Capacity Building and actions suggested by the research group. First, develop the school by focusing on strengths using a program like StrengthsFinder 2.0 or VIA Character Strengths (Niemiec, 2013). Develop teams and professional learning communities based on information from the strength's programs. Work on developing the school's culture by creating as many authentic leadership positions as possible and giving autonomy in decision making. Trust the staff.

Everyone deserves and benefits from coaching and mentoring. Ensure that the very best teachers are provided the same opportunities for growth as less proficient staff. Schools and school systems will thrive when we build capacity by first hiring the very best candidates who aspire to lead in alignment with the core values and then providing them the opportunity to develop into experts in their field.

PART 3: CONCLUSIONS AND CALL TO ACTION

Edward Deming summarized the importance and power of a system and people's strengths through an example using his love of music. His summary highlights the focus of the chapter succinctly.

> In rare moments when he was not pursuing his mission, Deming polished his skills as an organist and music composer. His version of the national anthem, which addresses people's inability to hit all the notes, serves as a metaphor for one of his points for management: don't blame the singers (workers) if the song is written poorly (the system is the problem); instead, rewrite the music (fix the system). In life and in art, Deming simply wanted to make it easier for people to sing. (The W. Edwards Deming Center for Quality, Productivity, and Competitiveness, 2022)

It was gleaned from the research group that having a vision of what the school can become while understanding the connections between subsystems developed hope and trust in the shared possibilities. Positive and aligned subsystems stimulate energy for the overall system. Never underestimate the potential for excellence that can be achieved by using personal, team, department, and school strengths and by making sure that the subsystems are integrated, interconnected, and thus interdependent.

The knowledge of networks and the importance of relationships creates an understanding that prohibits working in isolation. Positive communication is achieved by being out in the school and having as many conversations with people as possible. Consistency of leadership and staff retention over time were factors in every school serving students from impoverished situations that achieved remarkable success. The deeper our understanding of all the components that make up the whole system, the closer we come to the reality of coherence.

Two interviewees discussed appreciative strategies that were almost like magic because of how much success they were achieving. Though this study does not identify any magical feats; it links the application of appreciative strategies to positive success in schools. In summary, we have learned that the major themes of strengths, vision, purpose, core values, relationships, and generative communication, were complex and critical to the success of a school's major systems and subsystems. Each point highlighted in the study should be considered an idea that could lead to greater unity of purpose and coherence.

CALL TO ACTION

AOE and whole system coherence are needed to retain educators and secure a sustainable future that survives and flourishes. Every leader can take appreciative steps in each major system, subsystem, and interaction to support work to achieve whole system coherence.

There are many questions left unanswered: Where do we begin the quest to reach whole system coherence? What areas and ideas have the most significant effect on my journey to develop an appreciative school? Will the everyday demands and external forces ever allow the leader to experience the joy of leadership? Add questions and start on a career-long journey to whole system coherence, knowing that establishing an appreciative and sustainable school is possible. This is systems thinking in action.

REFERENCES

Barrett, F., & Fry, R. (2005). *Appreciate inquiry: A positive approach to building cooperative capacity*. Taos Institute Publications.

Burrello, L., Beitz, L., & Mann, J. (2016). *A positive manifesto: How appreciative schools can transform public education*. Elephant Rock Books.

Collins, J. C., & Porras, J. L. (1996). Building your company's vision. *Harvard Business Review*, 65–77.

Cooperrider, D., & Whitney, D. (2005). *Appreciative inquiry: A positive revolution in change*. Berrett-Koehler Publishers, Inc.

Cooperrider, D., & Whitney, D. (2011). *The appreciative inquiry summit: An emerging methodology for whole system positive change.* Retrieved from https://www.davidcooperrider.com/wp-content/uploads/2011/10/The-AI-SummitMethodology-x.pdf

Goldberg, E. (2021, March 27). As pandemic upends teaching, fewer students want to pursue it. *New York Times.*

Hall, G. C. N. (2017, February 7). The Platinum Rule: Treat others the way they wish to be treated. *Psychology Today.*

Harigopal, K. (2006). *Management of organizational change: Leveraging transformation.* Response Books.

James, G. (n.d.). *99 inspiring tweets from Albert Einstein.* Retrieved from *Inc.* https://www.inc.com/geoffrey-james/99-inspiring-tweets-from-albert-einstein.html

Janse, B. (2019). *Appreciative leadership.* Retrieved from Tools Hero. https://www.toolshero.com/leadership/appreciative-leadership/

Mann, J. L., Roberts, L., & Burrello, L. C. (2018). *The journey of appreciative school leadership: A guide for strengths-based change.* Elephant Rock Books.

Merriam-Webster. (n.d.). Coherent. In *Merriam-Webster.com* dictionary. Retrieved March 31, 2022, from https://www.merriam-webster.com/dictionary/coherent

Niemiec, R. M. (2013, December 17). *VIA Survey or StrengthsFinder? Comparing the two most dominant strengths tests in the world.* Psychology Today. https://www.psychologytoday.com/us/blog/what-matters-most/201312/survey-or-strengthsfinder

Norton, J. D. (2022, February 6). *The quantum theory of waves and particles, Einstein for everyone.* https://sites.pitt.edu/~jdnorton/teaching/HPS_0410/chapters/quantum_theory_waves/index.html

Rath, T., & Conchie, B. (2008). *Strengths-based leadership: Great leaders, teams, and why people follow.* Gallup Press.

Schindler, J. (2018, December 19). *Your thoughts become your destiny.* Social Change, Social Justice. https://www.stangreensponcenter.org/2018/12/19/your-thoughts-become-your-destiny/

Sinek, S. (2009). *Start with why: How great leaders inspire everyone to take action.* Portfolio by Penguin Press.

Snyder, K. M., Johnson, M., & Snyder, K. J. (2021, November 8–10). Going hybrid on a dime: Lessons from schooling during the pandemic and implications for sustainable quality in education. Paper presented at the 14th Annual International Conference on Education, Research and Innovation, Sevilla, Spain [digital].

The W. Edwards Deming Center for Quality, Productivity, and Competitiveness (2022, February 2). *History.* https://www8.gsb.columbia.edu/deming/about/history

Walker, T. (2022, February 1). *Survey: Alarming number of educators may soon leave the profession.* NEA News. https://www.nea.org/advocating-for-change/new-from-nea/survey-alarming-number-educators-may-soon-leave-profession

Whitney, D., Trosten-Bloom, A., & Rader, K. (2010). *Appreciative leadership: Focus on what works to drive a winning performance and build a thriving organization.* McGraw-Hill.

Chapter Nine

Toward the School as a Sustainable Global Learning Center

John Fitzgerald and Elaine C. Sullivan

Over the past 30 years, the International School Connection (ISC) has invited school leaders to work with its worldwide network to develop the idea of schools as sustainable "global learning centers" (GLCs). In this time of complex learning demands on schools, the ISC has vigorously supported and demonstrated to educators how to adopt a more durable, resilient, and adaptive systems perspective for thinking about schooling. Leaders are encouraged to pay attention to the school as a whole system as it adapts to change and to create a working-together attitude toward a common purpose (Snyder et al., 2008).

This chapter aims to offer a way of thinking about school development through a global lens and to consider ways to foster students' global competence. The ISC's journey of development over the decades serves as a guide for a deliberate approach to integrating global realities into the school's daily life. It is hoped that the knowledge and understanding gained from this 30-year evolution will offer perspectives on a *systems thinking approach* to school development in these complex times.

Today's schools exist in an intensely unpredictable environment that needs to respond, adapt, and thrive by creating a positive learning environment. The ISC's vision for globalization crystallized over time into the view that "getting there" requires a view of the school as a "complex adaptive system" (CAS). The ISC now describes the school as a CAS because the parts are interdependent, and the individual components are networked to create a positive, energy-driven work environment, as defined by Holmes et al. (2013).

The perspective of the school responding as a living system, a CAS, helps participants understand and connect to how change occurs naturally. It is important as we fully understand the complexity of globalization on schooling, which calls for a fresh approach to school development. In "complexity theory," sustainability may be understood as a complex system adapting to environmental change over time (Snyder, 2019).

The ISC's story shares examples from four phases of its history on how a learning organization evolves to create a systemic development plan. During Phase 1, information is presented about networking and connecting school leaders worldwide to learn how schools might address the challenges of globalization and its stresses on schools. During this networking period, the ISC emerged as a global organization, which became a nonprofit in the United States.

In Phase 2, the ISC's expanding connection programs and networking opportunities increased discussions and its research efforts to learn about emerging global standards, which led to the creation of the *Global Learning Benchmarks* (GLBs). The benchmarking system became the foundation for future school development models and programs for addressing the global impact on schools. The third phase focused on creating a systemic school development model to guide schools to become globally oriented, called *Sustainable Schooling for a Global Age: High Touch and High Tech*, a model that was created by Karolyn Snyder (see Figure 9.1).

Eventually the ISC evolved into a more comprehensive approach for school change by merging the benchmarking system, the global context connecting schools to the outside world, with the emerging knowledge base about the most effective school development practices. In Phase 4, an energy metaphor from the complexity theories is introduced to motivate the school staff and others to participate in the change processes. The ISC's school development model expanded to include the GLBs, the UN Sustainable Development Goals, the PISA competencies, and UNESCO's citizenship standards for the sustainability of the school.

This story offers knowledge, insights, and observations on how to meet the challenges of integrating systems thinking and global benchmarking to continually adapt schools to changing times. The ISC's narrative is about organizational learning and becoming a complex adaptive system. Over time, the ISC began envisioning the school development process for an increased global orientation of schooling by thinking more systemically about whole system change, especially as external forces on schooling and living become more rapid and unpredictable.

PHASE 1: THE ISC'S ORGANIZATIONAL MODEL EMERGES

In the 1992 and 1993 Berlin and Sochi conferences, a group of European, North American, and South American professors, school principals, and school district leaders met to explore the possibilities of creating an international network to support school development. Later, in Stockholm, an agreement was made by three universities to support this international network and its efforts to address school change to the impact of globalization trends. The ISC connected its members digitally and face-to-face to support professional development for principals and research on school development (Snyder & Acker-Hocevar, 2003).

The focus was on examining the school's local environment in the context of global forces to facilitate school development. A formal organizational structure evolved to include an international online community, annual meetings, and school partnerships. The world was becoming increasingly networked, which provided the focus for the ISC programs. It was challenging to design an organizational system built on networks that could serve to connect educational leaders around the world in new digital learning communities (Snyder et al., 2008).

ISC Global Summit Conferences

Over the decades, the ISC held annual global summits in a city of its members' countries, including Sweden, Finland, Russia, Norway, Canada, Venezuela, United States, and China. Summit participants joined in leadership lectures, study groups, discussions, and school visits to observe local efforts to address school change due to the impact of globalization. These early summits were significant building blocks in the ISC's growth by solidifying the ISC's role as an international facilitator and leader around emerging global features and school change. The ISC conferences generated knowledge and information about the effects of globalization in schools.

A consistent organizational identity also emerged from local hub level members' discussions, which helped to clarify the ISC's aims, mission, and purpose, which were approved during the 2003 Helsinki Conference. The ISC's *aim* is for students to become competent and caring citizens within a global society. The ISC's *mission* is to promote sustainable schooling for a global age of living and working. The ISC's *purpose* is to offer services advocating a systemic, sustainable approach to school development connected to a global learning orientation framed by the ISC's Global Learning Benchmarks.

ISC developed several essential programs and processes for connecting worldwide that extended its capacity to further communicate and connect among its members. Some of these include (1) international global hubs; (2) advanced graduate degree programs; (3) international school partnerships; (4) international school study visits and teacher exchanges; and (5) ISC international youth conferences. The following section briefly describes the programs for carrying out the ISC's aims, mission, and purpose and in providing more structure to its organizational model.

ISC Global Hub Development

During a 2004 ISC Ottawa, Canada, conference, members decided to develop hubs of schools in ISC regions of the world to expand membership and support ISC activities. The ISC became a global learning network of hubs that included the United States, Canada, Spain, Sweden, Russia, China, and Finland (Snyder et al., 2008). The hubs' networking energy stimulated an increase in the types of connections, offering more opportunities to expand their globalization knowledge and ways to address globalization's impacts on schooling. The local hub connections resulted in more robust programs, supporting leadership and school development training.

Advanced Degree Programs

In 2000, university officials signed a multi-national/multi-university partnership between Mid-Sweden University, Linkoping University, and the University of South Florida during the ISC global summit in Stockholm. Online master's and doctoral degree programs were created by the University of South Florida, called *Global Organizational Development*, which included online courses and annual face-to-face work during the annual ISC global summit. These advanced degree programs became the first fully online graduate programs at the University of South Florida.

Participants worked together digitally in international learning communities to gain information about the impact of globalization on schools and the importance of networking to learn how to handle needed change. This teaching and learning structure became the foundation for the ISC's growing role as a facilitator providing educational learning experiences for principals in an expanding global age.

International School Partnerships

For more than 30 years, ISC's school partnerships thrived and enhanced partners' ability to communicate across national boundaries and share cultural similarities and differences. Snyder and Acker-Hocevar (2003) highlighted how school partnerships, as well as the cross-border social networking of school leaders in a virtual environment, led to a greater understanding of the emerging "digital culture" in school organizations. These school partnerships began naturally, with teachers and students working together across time zones, discussing national cultures, popular culture, and common student interests.

Eventually, students addressed critical world issues, such as climate change, the environment, migrations, and water (Snyder et al., 2008). In 2006 a three-continent school partnership program was launched between schools in Stockholm, Sweden, Pasco County, Florida (United States), and Shenzhen, China, with over 50 schools participating (Snyder et al., 2010). This ISC program was instrumental in expanding a global understanding of cultures and schooling, and ways of seeing the world.

The communication experiment of using new technology began in 2001 with Web CT's learning platform (Wagenius & Snyder, 2002). In 2009–2010, ISC had many schools connected in partnership programs using Skype and other digital media to learn in online communities (Snyder, 2014). These partnership programs were essential for ISC members to learn to use evolving and new technologies (Snyder et al., 2008). Partnership communications occur now in many formats, such as WeChat, FaceTime, WhatsApp, and Zoom.

International School Study Visits

The purpose of the study visits was to enable teachers and principals to explore and study the differences and similarities between their schools, and to study a global challenge. In 1999 the first study group of ISC principals visited various school locations in Sweden, with individual visitors paired with Swedish principals to visit and study their schools. After several days, all involved returned to the Stockholm Summit to debrief and discuss what they had learned.

Two other study visits occurred during the Sochi and Beijing Summits with groups using an ISC study guide to enhance learning and understanding about schooling and its impact. The Summit in Sochi concluded with several cultural and celebratory feasts unique to the area. A bus trip explored cultural locations in China, with many citizens participating in recreational and cultural activities. The visitors reported a greater awareness of the global impact on schooling.

Teacher Exchange Study Visit

The purpose of the study visits was for teachers to learn from other teachers about how they operated in their schools and about the culture of the other's country. A study visit took place in 2003 between the Ottawa-Carleton,

Canada, and Katrineholm, Sweden, school districts, followed by a 2004 return visit. Thirty Swedish teachers came to Ottawa to live and work in classrooms with a partner teacher for one week, ending with a debriefing of stories and data about the experience.

All 60 educators reported that this was a significant professional and cultural learning experience. The sponsoring school districts and the ISC received a written report about the exchange. This feedback helped shape future ISC exchanges in working with large groups seeking to share their craft and culture for managing change due to the dynamics of globalization (Fitzgerald, 2004).

International Youth Conferences

Teachers requested the creation of a youth school connections program for students to learn about globalization and other students' cultures. These connections evolved into three International Youth Summits for middle and high school students in Tampa, Beijing, and Nykoping, Sweden. Each conference focused on different UN Sustainable Development Goals (SDGs); for example, the Swedish conference highlighted the UN goal of *water sustainability*. After this point, the ISC determined that the UN SDGs and PISA Competencies needed to be included with the GLBs as dimensions of the ISC's school development model.

Phase 1 Insights

The ISC, through its involvement with many international partners, developed as a global influence and resource for school development. Phase 1 enabled the ISC as an organization to mature and develop multiple global programs based on its aim, mission, and purpose. The ISC programs provided learning and growth opportunities for educators by simply connecting schools across borders. These connections with the ISC support led to learning about other cultures, school responses to globalization, viewing and appreciating how other teachers worked, and gaining general knowledge about the impact of globalization.

The ISC grew from these experiences worldwide and began to take a broader and deeper view of how change and school development occurs. In addition, as the ISC gained more expertise and knowledge from its connections, it began to view schooling from a more systemic global perspective and promoted sustainable school development. These experiences all became the "stepping stones" for how the ISC began to grow its school development process toward achieving the vision of preparing students for global living.

PHASE 2: THE EMERGENCE OF THE ISC GLOBAL LEARNING BENCHMARKS

At the 2004 Ottawa Summit, discussions in a committee environment led ISC members to develop Global Learning Benchmarks for schools to use as a guide for creating a global learning center approach to schooling. During Phase 2, the benchmarks became the central focus of ISC's global school development programs. Ottawa hub members developed each benchmark further, producing a set of descriptors known as *characteristics*. At the 2005 Madrid Summit, hosted by the Spanish hub, members explored emerging global challenges and also approved the idea of the Global Learning Benchmarks and their characteristics.

The GLC Benchmarks Validation

The ISC leadership team facilitated an exchange of ideas and perspectives among all hub members and school leaders regarding possible benchmarks that groups worldwide could support. The community provided feedback for clarity, importance, and comprehension of potential benchmarks. After a period of dialogue and clarification about a successful school's characteristics, ten main ideas emerged to become the ISC's Ten Global Learning Benchmarks.

A formal validation study was conducted among worldwide ISC members (Sullivan, 2006). The benchmarks marked the beginning of a common language for describing a school with a global learning orientation, which also identified best practices for observing responsive, globally oriented schools (Snyder, 2019). The benchmarks focused on school change decisions across divisions and subject boundaries, encouraging group decision making and action planning.

The GLC Benchmarks

There are two benchmark divisions: (1) learning about the global learning environment and (2) preparing for success in the global environment (Snyder et al., 2008). The following list defines the characteristics of each benchmark under the respective divisions.

I. The Global Learning Environment for Students Cluster

GLB 1: The curriculum provides opportunities to learn about local and global forces that influence change.

GLB 2: The school as a growing system has a vision and a plan to connect with the global community and its dynamic forces.
GLB 3: Educators participate in professional development activities in a globally networked environment to promote learning.
GLB 4: Partnerships with local, regional, and other global businesses enhance the direction of school development.
GLB 5: The school annually shows evidence of improving or sustaining student performance levels, using multiple local, regional, or international measures.

II. Student Preparation for Success in a Global Environment Cluster

GLB 6: Current knowledge about human learning guides teaching and learning practices throughout the school.
GLB 7: International projects or programs are included in the school's curriculum to promote global learning opportunities for all students.
GLB 8: Students are developing capacities for success in the evolving global workforce, which includes emerging technologies.
GLB 9: Students learn and use democratic decision-making processes that value diversity and promote equity and the appreciation for human life as foundations for becoming global citizens.
GLB 10: Students demonstrate an orientation for caring about the human community and its sustainable development.

In 2018, Corbett Preparatory School of IDS in Tampa, Florida, created a brochure of the Global Learning Benchmarks (GLBs) and Characteristics to globalize the school's curriculum and learning activities. The publication served as a guide for the school staff in its initial approaches to implementing the benchmarks to create a more globally oriented school. Corbett Prep and the ISC leadership team used the GLB brochure to assist other schools in learning how to globalize their school development process.

The Global Learning Benchmarking System Model

In 2005 the ISC leadership team designed a *Global Learning Benchmarking System* for schools to become certified as global learning centers. The Global Learning Benchmarks and Characteristics became a guide for the school's self-study and certification review, in a portfolio format, outlining a school's program strengths and needs from a global curricular, pedagogical, and socio-organizational perspective. The review gave a school an ongoing measure of its globally oriented activities and its preparation for adapting to local and global conditions that provide information to initiate innovation (Sullivan, 2019).

The first certified ISC-GLC school was the A. Y. Jackson Secondary School in Ottawa, soon followed by A. J. Ferrell Middle School and the Corbett Preparatory School in Tampa. These GLC-certified schools became models for others in pursuing a global learning center approach to learning. The GLB system was so effective and practical in its use with certification-seeking schools that the ISC extended the benchmarking system for all member schools to guide school change. The global benchmarking process became the core of the ISC's school development planning.

The GLB approach for intentionally guiding school improvement became the foundation for future iterations of the ISC's school development model. The ISC continued to recognize globalization as a significant impactor in determining curricular change. The benchmarking system became the strategic driver for planning change. The GLBs provided a lens to assist students to become active in a global society. The GLBs were the framework that glued together the school development process in a continuous cycle, enabling leaders to think systemically about school change holistically (Sullivan, 2006).

The GLB Professional Development Programs

A new training program for school and school district leaders, called Leadership for Sustainable School Development (LSSD), was created to meet the needs of school leaders who are interested in facilitating school development for sustainable futures (Snyder, 2017). Based on the Managing Productive Schools Training Program (Snyder, 1988) and the Global Learning Center Benchmarks, the LSSD program provided a systemic orientation to school development. The focus was on building collaborative work cultures to generate motivational energy to achieve school sustainability within a globally benchmarked context and digital culture.

The Benefits of the Global Learning Benchmarks for School Development

The most powerful benefit of using the Global Learning Benchmarks tool has been to align all school development decisions systemically. In the school development processes, the benchmarks become a guide for the vision of school development to determine where change is necessary and a way of aligning organizational structures, processes, and work culture.

The GLBs are also an enabler for staff to shape and maintain the consistency of its vision and congruence of the interrelated parts, and a way to develop a global orientation for the school's curriculum and the development of instructional activities to create a culture of learning. These GLB benefits ultimately encouraged using a systems perspective when considering school development to effect change for the overall school, ensuring sustainability (Sullivan, 2006).

PHASE 3: A CHANGE OF DIRECTION—SCHOOL DEVELOPMENT FOR SUSTAINABLE SCHOOLING

In its local and worldwide work with school leaders, the ISC recognized many developing trends on how schools work more effectively to address change. In 2017, the ISC decided to include the new organizing work trends for planning school change instead of only considering a global orientation by the GLB system as in earlier collaborations. The eight trends in schools with a strong global orientation provided additional clarity to change processes within the overall school system (Snyder, 2019).

The trends include (1) real-life challenges as a force for local and global development; (2) common goals and different tasks that drive action; (3) individual learning goals that connect to community/classroom goals; (4) interdependent learning teams that evolve and change naturally; (5) information and technology that create rich learning environments; (6) multiple global resources and partnership projects that stimulate student interest; (7) creative and critical thinking that become a way of life; and (8) self-assessment using world-class standards.

These characteristics offered a complete context for systemically considering the school as an interconnected system. The identified thriving schools provide pathways to a more responsive and globally oriented change process. The trends provide a complete and clearer picture for decisions. The ISC's school development model uses these trends to focus on the whole and the interactions and interrelationships of the parts when analyzing information to determine needed change. Further, this new knowledge helps faculty make decisions through a "systems" lens to understand how the parts work together for choosing the best leverage point.

Sustainable Schooling for a Global Age: High Touch–High Tech

The ISC's benchmarking system for school change evolved to include a broader context of globalization, creating increasing global demands beyond the school as a system. This updated thinking into a new model, called Sustainable Schooling for a Global Age: High Touch–High Tech, which is

Sustainable Schooling for a Global Age:
Leading the School's Growth as an Integrated Complex System

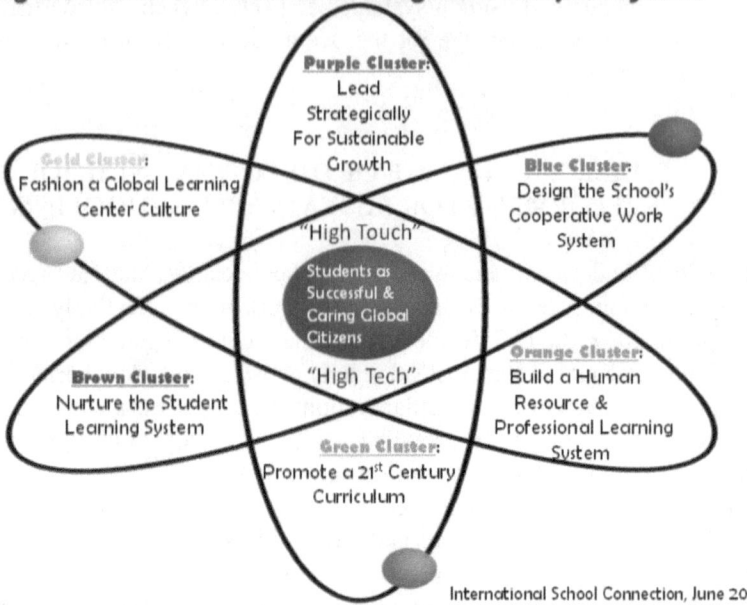

Figure 9.1. Sustainable Schooling for a Global Age (SSGA): High Touch–High Tech. *Karolyn Snyder, International School Connection, 2019.*

built upon new patterns of organizations as living systems, and change that is driven by principles from complexity and chaos theories (Snyder, 2017).

The model in Figure 9.1 reflects a holistic view of a dynamic orbital system with six connected revolving satellites representing various work processes that form a ring around a core centerpiece representing student learning. These new work patterns included (1) strategic leadership; (2) organizational planning—a cooperative work system; (3) a human resource and professional learning system; (4) a 21st century curriculum that includes academic, artistic, social, emotional, and physical learning; (5) a culture for learning and growth; and (6) cultural integration of global learning (Snyder, 2017).

A school's perspective on how to connect the school organization to its external environment is crucial for preparing students for the future. The six interdependent work processes and behaviors briefly are described as follows:

1. *Strategic Leadership:* The critical leadership challenge is to continuously identify disequilibrium, see opportunities for change in the school's external and internal environments, and understand their impact on its development (Snyder, 2017).

2. *Organizational Planning:* A Cooperative Work System promoting a high-performing work culture where school leaders, staff, and other community members identify a vision and together study the changing environment, identifying improvement targets while assessing improvement. Cooperation becomes the norm in this work culture (Snyder & Anderson, 1986).
3. *Human Resources and Professional Learning:* A sustainable school is built over time by (a) employing people who strengthen the school's work culture, (b) continuously developing a high-performance culture by providing ongoing attention to professional learning, and (c) developing a human resource and professional learning system (Snyder & Anderson, 1986).
4. *21st Century Curriculum:* Sustainable education is promoted when knowledge is pursued topically in an interdisciplinary fashion to address the academic, the arts, the humanities, and physical skills, as well as social and emotional capacities (Snyder, 2017).
5. *Student Learning System*: Teachers provide growth goals while working in teams with students learning together, independently, and in multi-aged environments (Snyder, 2017).
6. *A Global Learning Culture:* Fosters global learning while teachers identify global trends and the challenges of disequilibrium in the world, which point out areas where growth and change are needed, and then connect to resources to help gain solutions (Snyder et al., 2008).

The above model of sustainable school development illustrates the significant role of the ISC's benchmarks in the school development process as a cohesive support system for schools to respond to changing conditions and the increasingly complex demands of a global society.

The Corbett GLB Integration Project: Purpose, Implementation, and Research

In 2016, the ISC leadership team recognized the exceptional progress made by Corbett Preparatory School of IDS in Tampa as a global learning center. The school had become effective in "systems thinking" in most of its work structures as it continuously integrated the latest pedagogical innovations into its practices. The ISC examined how its school development model might attain a "value-added" perspective as a systems thinking approach to school development. It was felt that a school or district that focused on the systemic interdependence, interrelationships, and interconnections of its parts would increase school sustainability.

In 2017–2018, an ISC/Corbett Prep collaboration sought to increase the global orientation of the school's work structures. The project envisioned developing students' global competence and citizenship. The ISC studied the implementation to gain more effective and efficient insight for integrating the GLBs into all learning activities and structures. The GLC Benchmark Project provided preparation and support for staff members to integrate the GLBs into classroom lessons and activities. The goal was to use the benchmarks to nurture student competence and increase the global orientation for all school activities (Sullivan, 2019).

Over the project year, the school and ISC leaders observed more GLB integration and thoughtfulness in lesson planning and instruction, and in everyday school life activities. The project's activities created conversations and individual teacher reports about how to connect lessons to the Global Learning Benchmarks. Focus group discussions revealed a variety of approaches to achieving success with the challenge of integrating the benchmarks into classroom life. Clearer understandings of the GLBs and their use as guides emerged, establishing a more intentional use in the school development process (Sullivan, 2019).

PHASE 4: THE NEXT STEP—USING AN ENERGY SYSTEM MODEL FOR ISC'S SCHOOL DEVELOPMENT

A systems analysis of the GLB integration project's findings showed new knowledge about the natural energy needed to drive school change. The analysis indicated how this information might help others know how to create processes and structures to create networking and collaboration for self-organization. A new perspective of how to handle school change came from the synthesis of research, project data, the ISC team's mental models, knowledge about change, and the integration of GLB into the school development system.

In Phase 4, the ISC's school development processes were supported by a platform that included the global context, global competencies, and global citizenship development. This platform brings systemic consistency to a school's daily life, increasing schooling sustainability. The school development platform to be more relevant and comprehensive includes the 2030 UN Sustainable Development Goals, PISA's global competencies, the ISC's GLBs, UNESCO's citizenship standards, and new global work patterns.

The ISC blended these components to create a comprehensive system described by Snyder (2019) in the *ISC Global Learning Platform for Sustainable Schooling.* Snyder's Human Energy System Model presented in Chapter

1 supports the change process. The ISC story illustrates how schools can apply this energy system to develop sustainable practices that integrate current needs with future challenges.

A new narrative suggests that a relationship exists between the school development process and the school as a system, where the development process is the catalyst for energy creation. The school is seen as the entity that responds as a "complex adaptive system." The system creates energy through connections with others to facilitate and fuel desirable change. A positive self-sustaining energy system in place aids the process of moving toward a school's systemic change. The ISC record shows how schools can apply the Human Energy System Model to develop sustainable practices that combine current needs with future challenges.

CALL TO ACTION

The ISC challenges school leaders to consider transforming their schools into sustainable global learning centers using the ISC Global Learning Platform for Sustainable Schooling. The challenges of sustainability and the importance of a systems view are critical in integrating all elements of globalization into the school's organizing work processes.

This ISC story promotes school development as the global trends impact the purposes of schooling and how students might be prepared for their future in uncertain conditions. School leaders can integrate global learning activities into school life, such as school partnerships, teacher exchanges, school visits, and ongoing professional development for global initiatives. The ISC story provides insights, knowledge, and resources to meet the challenges of sustainable schooling. Be mindful and learn on the way. Enjoy the journey!

REFERENCES

Fitzgerald, J. (2004). *The Katrineholm / Ottawa Sweden teacher exchange study visit.* An ISC report, the Katrineholm School District and the Ottawa School District. Ottawa, Ontario.

Holmes, K., Clement, J., & Albright, J. (2013). The complex task of leading educational changes in schools. *School Leadership and Management, 33*(3), 270–283.

Shaked, H., & Schechter, C. (2017). *Systems thinking for school leaders: Holistic leadership for excellence in education.* Springer.

Snyder, K. J. (1988). *Competency training for managing productive schools.* Academic Press. Harcourt, Brace, & Jovanovich.

Snyder, K. J. (2017). *Sustainable schooling for a global age*. Retrieved from www.iscnow.org.

Snyder, K. J. (2019). Sustainable schooling for a global age: Preparing globally competent students: The K–12 schooling challenge. In W. B. James & C. Cobanoglu (Eds.), *Advances in global education and research*, Vol. 3, 136–149. University of South Florida Press.

Snyder, K. J. (2021). Building sustainable systems for schooling in turbulent times: Big ideas from the sciences. In J. Glanz (Ed.), *Crisis and pandemic leadership: Implications for meeting the needs of students, teachers, and parents*. Roman & Littlefield Publishers.

Snyder, K. J., Acker-Hocevar, M., & Snyder, K. M. (2000, 2008). *Living on the edge of chaos: Leading schools into the global age*. ASQ Quality Press.

Snyder, K. J., & Anderson, R. (1986). *Managing productive schools: Toward an ecology*. Harcourt, Brace, Jovanovich.

Snyder, K. J., Mann, J. I., Johnson, E., & Xing, M. (2010, Fall). Schools without borders: The global partnership project. *Innovation Magazine*.

Snyder, K. M. (2014). Concept mapping, voice thread, visual images: Helping teachers spawn divergent thinking and dialogic learning. In L. Shedletsky & J. Beaudry (Eds.), *Cases on teaching and critical thinking through visual representation strategies*. IGI Global Publishers.

Snyder, K. M., & Acker-Hocevar, M. (2003). Building international cultures of synergy through online social networks. In F. Kochran (Ed.), *International perspectives on mentoring*. Information Age Press.

Sullivan, E. (2006). *Validation study of the ISC ten benchmarks*. International School Connection, Inc.

Sullivan, E. (2019). The ISC global learning benchmark integration project at Corbett Prep: A case study. *2019 Global Conference on Education and Research (GLO-CER)* Proceedings Book, ID 257. University of South Florida Press.

Wagenius, M., & Snyder, K. M. (2002). Building international education networks with ICT: Possibilities and challenges. In J. Perhoff (Ed.), *Internationalization in a shrinking world*. Books on Demand Press.

About the Editors and Contributors

Karolyn J. Snyder, EdD, for over 50 years, has served education as a teacher, school leader, professor, and president of the International School Connection, Inc. With over 300 publications and professional work in 40 countries, her work has been grounded in a systems approach to school development, as well as newer developments in physics that offer guidance for leading school change over time. Over the last 30 years, Snyder has also worked with schools and universities around the world to prepare students as competent and caring global citizens.

Kristen M. Snyder, PhD, is professor in quality management and associate professor in education at Mid Sweden University. She has contributed to school and leadership development internationally through a variety of programs including the International School Connection. She was the vice president for research in the International School Connection. She is the author of numerous publications on leadership and innovation in schools, and co-authored *Living on the Edge of Chaos: Leading Schools into the Global Age.*

Michele Acker-Hocevar, PhD, professor emeritus of Washington State University (WSU), is a scholar of organizational behavior and theory. Her career spans over 45 years in public school teaching and administration, university teaching, and administration culminating as vice chancellor of academic affairs. She was an editor of the *International Journal of Leadership in Education* (IJLE) and is co-lead of a national study of superintendents and principals, sponsored by the University Council of Educational Administration.

Robert H. Anderson, PhD, was a Harvard professor and dean of the College of Education at Texas Tech University, who became known as the father of team teaching and multi-aged classrooms, causing a revolution in how schools are organized today. His work took him around the world to influence the quality of school learning and school organizations with his breakthrough ideas about focusing on student success as the major purpose of schooling. His work on coaching teachers, primarily as they work in teams, led to a new vital field of inquiry known as clinical supervision. His impact on the quality and direction of education has left an impact. Anderson died in 2010 at the age of 92.

John Fitzgerald, PhD, has worked as a teacher, consultant, principal, district supervisor, and superintendent with three Ontario school districts in Canada. He has designed and coordinated the Principal's Qualification Program at the University of Ottawa. For 37 years he was an instructor and instructor trainer with Performance Learning Systems (PLS) and served as adjunct graduate professor with Drake University in Iowa and Leslie College in Massachusetts. He also served as vice president for development and cochair of the board of directors for the International School Connection (ISC).

John Mann, EdD, is a senior Anchin Center director for leadership development and retired instructor of educational leadership and policy studies at the University of South Florida. His long career has included the principalship, director of leadership development, and assistant superintendent of curriculum and instructional services in Pasco County School District, Florida (United States). He has presented over 100 leadership training events and keynote addresses. John is most proud of his research focus on appreciative inquiry and appreciative organizing in public schools as it applies to developing positive and sustainable organizations.

Anna Mårtensson is a PhD student and junior lecturer in quality management at Mid Sweden University, Sweden. She previously worked as a development coordinator for quality in schools and preschools at the municipal level. Her areas of research include quality culture in organizations and the practice of quality that supports the UN sustainability goals.

David Scanga, EdD, earned a bachelor's degree in psychology, a master's degree in educational psychology, and a doctorate in educational leadership and policy studies. His career in public and international education spans 42 years working in various roles: school psychologist, principal, and assistant superintendent. Currently, Dr. Scanga is an adjunct professor of educational leadership at Saint Leo University.

Renee Sedlack, EdD, has a doctorate degree in educational leadership and policy studies. For 41 years she served as a teacher, assistant principal, principal, and human resources director. Dr. Sedlack is an associate professor of educational leadership at Saint Leo University. Her research interest is in discovering ways to close the achievement gap among underserved youth.

Elaine C. Sullivan, EdD, a 38-year public school leader in Florida, was recognized as the U.S. 1998 National High School Principal of the Year and the 1997 Florida Principal of the Year. Sullivan created ISC youth initiatives and chaired the ISC Global Benchmark and Global Learning Center programs. Dr. Sullivan developed the Quantum Strategic School Leadership Model.

www.ingramcontent.com/pod-product-compliance
Lightning Source LLC
Chambersburg PA
CBHW020418230426

43663CB00007BA/1214